God Trusted
a Woman

Leadership Lessons from the Life
of Dr. Frances M. Alguire,
First Laywoman to Lead the World Methodist Council

As told to Cynthia B. Astle

Acknowledgements

Writing a biography of a living person offers a rare and wonderful opportunity to capture someone's life story while they're still here to tell it. For this reason, Frances and Donald Alguire head this list of acknowledgements. The extraordinary lives they've lived and shared together, their meticulous record-keeping, Don's extensive photograph collection, and their patience and persistence have guided every step of this unique history telling how a country girl from a farm in Michigan became the first laywoman to serve as the leader of World Methodism. All photographs in this book are by Donald Alguire or from the Alguire Family collection unless otherwise credited.

In addition, Frances Alguire's colleagues, family and friends made invaluable contributions by writing personal remembrances for this biography. They include: Catherine Alguire, Mary Alguire Papish, Vivian Miner, Jean Beal, Dr. Monica Attias of the Community of Sant'Egidio, Andris Y. Salter, Esther Jadhav and Bishop Jesse and Annamary DeWitt, and colleagues from The World Methodist Council: Dr. Joe Hale, General Secretary emeritus; Dr. George Freeman, General Secretary; Dr. John C.A. Barrett, 2006-2011 Chair; His Eminence Sunday Mbang, 2001-2006 Chair; Mary Um, Board of Social Responsibility & Laity of the Korean Methodist Church; Dr. H. Eddie Fox, World Evangelism Director; Ralph C. Young, 1986-2001 Geneva Secretary; Dr. Denis C. Dutton, 2001-2006 Geneva Secretary; Rev. Dr. Hal Brady, 1996-2001 Program Chair; Linda Greene, former Executive Assistant to Dr. Hale; Mary Ellen Bullard, past member of the Executive Committee; Dr. William K. Quick, past Associate General Secretary for development; Dr. Gustavo Jacques Diaz Alvim, 2001-2006 Presidium member.

Finally, I would like to express my personal gratitude for the love and support of my husband, John Astle, and our son, Sean Damon Astle. Both of them took over household duties and gave up family time to allow me to write and edit this book. In particular, John, a digital publishing expert, helped with the final technical details, while Sean, a writer himself, supplied regular encouragement for me to "keep on keeping on" when work went slowly. They are God's dearest blessings to me in this life.

This book is a tribute to the contributions of all these generous souls whose lives have been touched by God's grace channeled through Dr. Frances M. Alguire.

Cynthia B. Astle, Dallas, Texas, October, 2007

Foreword

By Joe Hale
General Secretary Emeritus
World Methodist Council

My introduction to Frances and Donald Alguire came through what I heard and learned regarding their ecumenical work in the city of Chicago.

Bishop Paul Washburn appointed Fran to membership on the World Methodist Council. Her appointment coincided with my nomination to become General Secretary at the 13th World Methodist Council and Conference (1976) in Dublin, Ireland. My nomination had been screened previously by a search committee in New York, a meeting of the Council Executive Committee in Accra, Ghana, and a Nominating Committee in London prior to election at the world meeting.

I soon came to know that Fran Alguire possessed gifts which few people have. She was eager to celebrate the gifts of others, was open to different perspectives and cultures, and had a leadership style that first and foremost appreciated the gifts of other people, and then built consensus effectively.

Over the 25 years I was privileged to work with her, I realized the work she did and the prominence she achieved was never something she sought for personal recognition. This observation was confirmed looking back from the time we first met in Dublin in 1976 to the time we concluded our respective service – she as World Methodist Council President and I as General Secretary in Brighton, England, in 2001.

Bishop Dwight Loder, who was serving as President of the North American Section in 1976, knew Fran, and saw her as a person possessing unique gifts that could mean much to the Council's future. Loder nominated her to the World Methodist Council Executive Committee. She was elected, and her first meeting in this capacity was the 1981 World Methodist Conference in Honolulu, Hawaii.

Five years later, in Nairobi, Kenya, Fran Alguire was nominated and elected president of the North American Section of the World Methodist Council. North America was a significant area in Methodism worldwide, having a membership of just over 24 million and a community of 52 million worldwide at the time.

Bishop William R. Cannon, who had a long history and association with the World Methodist Council and had served in many key leadership roles, also saw Fran Alguire's potential. In 1995, at a meeting of an important Council committee on the campus of Cambridge University in England, during one of the breaks, Bishop Cannon put his hand on Fran's shoulder and said, "Fran, I've given this much thought, and you are the one to lead the World Methodist Council." He then told her the story of his own service, as a Council member, on the WMC Executive Committee, as President of the North American Section, and then Chair of the World Presidium. Fran was taken aback by what he said to her, and replied, "Yes, but after that there is a lot of difference in us!"

Fran Alguire was later nominated to lead the world organization. She was elected in 1996 as the first woman to head the world body since it was conceived and began with the first Conference in London, England, in 1881.

Her Presidency was visionary, and opened doors to undreamed-of accomplishments:

> * The expansion of the World Headquarters complex, with adjacent property purchased, and the building of a magnificent replica of the Old Rectory in Epworth, England, made possible by a gift of $1.5 million from Jane and Royce Reynolds. The full-scale model of the "home of the Wesleys" in Epworth, England stands today beside the World Methodist Museum on the shore of Lake Junaluska in North Carolina.
>
> * The establishment of a major endowment for the World Methodist Council.
>
> * The designing of a unique "historic Methodism" event in 1988, while she was President of the North American Section, enabling several hundred people to retrace their Methodist roots in England. Two trains, leased from British Rail, took people to visit the actual places where the story of John Wesley and the Methodist movement happened: London, Epworth, York, Gloucester and Brighton, with visits to, and a worship

service, at each site. The two trains, named "The John
Wesley" and "The Charles Wesley," sped from London in
opposite directions with some 500 passengers on each
train.

Always with a view of the larger picture, Dr. Alguire envisioned a
program at the turn of the Millennium from 1999 to 2000, to be held
in the Old City of Jerusalem. I invited church leaders who came to the
Old City from a number of countries for consultation. Meetings were
scheduled with various Bishops, Heads of Churches and other religious
leaders. Memorable events were staged at historic biblical sites and in
Jerusalem and Bethlehem.

One of the meetings in Jerusalem was with a Patriarch of one of the
Ancient Churches. His Palace and audience room was in an upper floor
of an ancient stone building in the walled Old City. The Patriarch, of
some age, was dressed in an impressive robe, with dazzling ecclesiastical
vestments, seated on an ornate throne set before walls adorned by glorious and ancient icons. Dr. Alguire was our leader and spokesperson at
the audience. At the close, she thanked the Patriarch, for receiving us.
She asked, "Your Holiness, may we have a prayer with you?" He replied:
"We pray in the Church!"

In 1976, the World Methodist Council established the World
Methodist Peace Award as an official decoration given annually for
extraordinary efforts made to further the cause of peace. The first award
was presented to an Irish woman, Saidie Patterson, for her efforts to halt
the sectarian violence between Catholics and Protestants in Northern
Ireland.

During Dr. Alguire's tenure, World Methodist Peace Awards were
given to:

    * The Community of Sant'Egidio, an international Catholic lay
association headquartered in Rome, for its efforts to negotiate
peace in a civil war in Mozambique;
    * Dr. Kofi A. Annan, Secretary General of the United Nations;
    * The Grandmothers of Plaza de Mayo in Buenos Aires,
Argentina, for their efforts to ascertain the fate of their "disap-
peared" relatives during the country's military dictatorship; and

Dr. Joe Hale and Dr. Frances Alguire flank Nelson Mandela at his investiture with the World Methodist Peace Award.

United Methodist News Service photo by Cynthia B. Astle
Courtesy of United Methodist Reporter

* Nelson Mandela, former president of the Republic of South Africa, in Capetown, South Africa, for bringing his nation peacefully out of the system of racial segregation known as apartheid.[1]

Other decorations created and presented to recognize service to the World Methodist Council during Fran's term were the Seat of Honor and the Order of Jerusalem, both awards for outstanding service to the World Methodist Council, presented at General Conferences of the member churches.

I will long remember one event when Dr. Alguire and I attended a major International Christian Youth Conference held at St. Simon's Island, Georgia. Dr. Alguire was scheduled to give the opening night's keynote address. Rain poured down, but as a part of the ceremony, a huge globe, representing the world, was to be lighted just outside the covered tabernacle. The youths trying to light the flame were soaking wet, and the flame itself burned off and on.

Undaunted, Fran opened her address to the world's Methodist youths that night by asking: "Who but Methodists would try to light the world on fire in the rain?"

This was what Dr. Frances Alguire did across World Methodism – light fires of hope and faith amid the rain of the world's woes. Those of us who witnessed her leadership saw the fire of God's Holy Spirit glow in her, and inspired by her, we saw how we could spread that sacred fire through our own lives and churches.

[1] Editor's note: Dr. Frances Alguire also presented the World Methodist Council Peace Award to the Rev. Dr. Joe Hale, at the World Methodist Conference meeting in Brighton, England, July 2001. According to Dr. Alguire: "As General Secretary of the World Methodist Council for 25 years, Joe Hale worked to ensure the voice of the Church was heard in opposition to apartheid, in endeavoring to reconcile national churches in conflict, and in promoting peace with justice in the Middle East."

Introduction
The Marks of a Leader
By Cynthia B. Astle

Some leaders are born, so we say, while others rise to lead in a crisis. Still others are trained from an early age in leadership skills. As the 21st Century moves along, our global society also is discovering that men and women lead in different, equally valid, styles, and that both styles will be required if our world is to prosper in the future.

In fact, it's often said these days that men's leadership stems from a "power over," or authoritarian model, while women's leadership emanates from a "power with," or communitarian model. Because the authoritarian model has been dominant for so long, the communitarian model – the "women's model" – often is seen as "soft," a euphemism for "ineffective" in the authoritarian context.

Yet there was nothing ineffective in the leadership style of Jesus, who sought to bring people into relationship with God and with one another, who welcomed women and others rejected or demeaned by society, who listened to others' needs and invited them into community. Frances Maxine Werner Alguire, the first laywoman to head the World Methodist Council, has been a leader in the style of Jesus.

In Dr. Alguire, the typical paths to leadership converged with her life and times, especially the rise of women's status and roles in Methodism, to produce an unusual, perhaps even unique, leader. Her eight decades of life and service demonstrate some key characteristics of the most successful Christian leaders.

Leaders put others first. In sharp contrast to many contemporary, self-centered lifestyles and theologies (even within the church), Frances Alguire directed herself toward the needs of others from an early age. From growing up on her family's farm in Michigan, to her career as a registered nurse, to her creativity and devotion as a homemaker, wife and mother, to her decades of faithful Christian service, she developed a keen sensitivity to others' needs. Her innate willingness to help, coupled with a strong intuition about what would best serve others, has enabled her through the years to initiate and foster progress that benefited many people – the mark of a leader.

Leaders listen to others. As remembrances and tributes to Frances came in for this book, one of her traits repeatedly noted by friends and colleagues was, "She's a good listener." Listening is a difficult skill to master, because the natural impulse is always to be thinking about what one will say next, rather than to set aside one's ego and genuinely hear what another person is saying. Listening takes practice, patience and self-emptying, a form of sacrifice – once again, characteristics of Jesus' leadership style.

Leaders invite others to participate. By the time she came to head the World Methodist Council, Frances Alguire had spent many years visiting countries around the world. While community plays an important role in most societies, leadership, even now, is often restricted to men. By fostering the participation of women, first among themselves, and then as equal partners in their societies, Dr. Alguire showed that all societies and institutions are stronger and more accomplished when all participate in decision-making.

Leaders cultivate relationships. Keeping up with family and friends takes effort, especially to maintain one's relationship with God. The church's most effective leaders, such as Frances Alguire, learn early on that no meeting, no sermon, no speech, no class, nothing is more important than daily time with God. It has been said that learning to be disciples of Jesus Christ is like playing the piano – unless we practice every day, we won't be ready when we're needed to play music. Dr. Alguire exemplifies this discipline.

Leaders are organized. Among her many gifts, Frances Alguire possesses an organizing skill surely the equal of Methodism's founder, John Wesley, who in turn was taught the value of daily discipline by his mother, Susanna Wesley. Yet organization in and of itself has no virtue unless it is directed toward something – unless it is genuine "ad-ministration," in the service of ministry. Whether one's ministry is making a nurturing home for one's family, or leading a church, or teaching, or any other vocation, the goal of organization is to accomplish a mission, a wisdom that Dr. Alguire has demonstrated consistently in her near-legendary management skills.

Leaders are lifelong learners. Frances Alguire's daughters once joked that long before their mother was honored with doctorates from two United Methodist institutions, she had accomplished her "LBD" degree – "learning by doing." Sometimes we in the church place too much emphasis on high academic degrees, depriving ourselves in the faith community of the wisdom learned through living every day. Over her lifetime, Frances never stopped adding to her skills, whether it was learning how to participate in a denominational board meeting, or what the customs were in a new country she was visiting. She has been open to learning from every experience, and willingly applied her practical education to leading World Methodism.

Leaders are persistent. Like all of us, Frances Alguire faced challenges in her life. When she was gravely injured in an accident as a young woman, she could have given up on her dream of becoming a registered nurse. When she was told there was no money to pay the expenses of a layperson to serve as chairwoman of the World Methodist Council, she could have said, "Well, then, no thank you." But she didn't give up; she found a way to make something happen.

Leaders take risks. Dr. Alguire often was the only woman – and a layperson at that – representing a global Christian communion among pope and patriarch, bishops and archbishops and other clergy. One can only imagine how startled people were to see her there, a petite, auburn-haired woman in everyday clothes among all the elaborately robed heads of churches. As at least one incident recounted in this book shows, those whose ministry includes upholding church tradition actively resisted her participation at times. In ways large and small, Frances Alguire risked crossing barriers and boundaries, something that Jesus himself did time and again.

Leaders shape, and are shaped by, the times in which they live. Frances Alguire would be a completely different person had she not grown up during the Great Depression, lived through World War II, raised her family during the 1950s and '60s, and come into national and international roles with the rise of the women's movement in the 1970s. At the same time, she has had a profound, and often unheralded, influence on the church and the world. Put another way, Christian leaders like Dr. Alguire live the time they're given to the fullest, and live their faith openly in the world.

Leaders tell stories. There were many reasons that Jesus taught in parables – stories. Partly, he told stories because that was how people thought and learned at the time. But he also told stories so that people might see themselves in new ways. As the late author Madeleine L'Engle once said, "Why does anybody tell a story? It does indeed have something to do with faith — faith that the universe has meaning, that our little human lives are not irrelevant, that what we choose or say or do matters, matters cosmically."

In this book, Frances Alguire has told the story of her life — the history of a woman leader whose choices and sayings and actions have mattered significantly to her family, her friends, her church and the world for eighty years. Her crowning leadership now is to share the wisdom of her lifetime with new generations of leaders. If you would be a leader for our times, learn from the life she has generously poured out for Christ and for the world that God loves.

Table of Contents

Chapter 1
'A Country Girl from a One-Room School'

The seeds of Frances Werner Alguire's global leadership were sown on her family's farm, near the rural village of LeRoy, located in the middle of Michigan's lower peninsula.

In the early morning hours of July 11, 1927, the sounds of a newborn infant could be heard. As Harold, the hired man for the Werner farm entered the kitchen he was surprised to hear a baby cry. He didn't recall being awakened during the night to drive the one-mile gravel road to fetch Harry Werner's sister-in-law, Gusta Ochs. At that moment, Gusta, mother of 13 children, was in the Werners' house helping Doctor Holmes deliver the second of Harry and Mary's four surviving children, another daughter.

The newborn's parents were still mourning the deaths of two children, Harriett Marie, born in 1924, and Maurice Robert, born in 1926. Their deaths in the first months of their lives told the tale of health care in the 1920s. In the time before penicillin, Harriett died from an infected navel. In the time before surgical miracles, Maurice died from complications of spina bifida.[1]

So her parents and five-year-old sister Kathryn rejoiced when a healthy baby girl, whom they named Frances Maxine Werner, entered the world. None of them could have imagined that this little girl, delivered by a country doctor and a neighboring aunt in her parents bedroom, would grow up to be known as Dr. Frances M. Alguire, the first laywoman to preside over the 70-million-strong World Methodist family.

Family traditions

The world into which Frances Maxine Werner was born seems idyllic from a 21st century perspective. America in 1927 was still predominantly a rural place, but times were changing. The 1920 invention of radio – termed "the farmer's friend" by scholars – was beginning to link farms and ranches across the country to a wider world. Farmers were able to get weather predictions and U.S. Department of Agriculture reports by radio, and radio stations begin developing programs around farmers' needs.[2]

Radio and the electricity that powered it took longer to get to central Michigan. It wasn't until the 1930s that electric power reached Michigan farms, followed by the establishment of radio station WKZO in Kalamazoo.

While their surrounding community may have been slower to get the marvels of progress, innovation was not new to the Werner family. Frances, her parents and siblings lived and worked on a farm founded by her paternal grandfather, John G. Werner, a German immigrant. Their home was a two-story brick, five-bedroom prairie-style structure that neighbors from the nearby village of LeRoy called "John's Folly."[3] Building his home in the early 1900s, Grandfather Werner outfitted the house with indoor plumbing on both floors, carbide-generated heat, and lights throughout, amenities that his less-visionary neighbors scorned as newfangled nonsense.

The farm prospered

"John's Folly" the house may have been, but the farm prospered. In addition to its well-equipped house, the Werner farm boasted a large cattle barn with a double hay loft, a chicken coop for three dozen laying hens and a sheep stable built on a hillside above the chicken coop. Two teams of horses, a dozen stalls for dairy cattle and pens for calves and yearlings filled the concrete-floored barn.[4]

Frances shared a birthday with her maternal grandfather, James Francis Bond, from whom she got her first name. Decades later, after novelist Ian Fleming turned his fictional spy into a worldwide phenomenon, Frances playfully introduced herself to new friends as "the granddaughter of James Bond – James F. Bond."[5]

Two years after she was born, Frances and her family welcomed her brother Forrest, and then sister Pauline two years after that. Kathryn, the oldest, and Pauline, the youngest, shared the same birthday, Feb. 8. When an inquisitive Frances remarked on the coincidence, her mother confessed: "Pauline was born just a few minutes before midnight on Feb. 7, but the doctor dated the birth certificate Feb. 8 when he made it out."

The greatest influences on Frances' early life were her siblings and her parents, Harry and Mary Werner. In a parallel to Susanna Wesley's instruction of her sons, John and Charles, the founders of Methodism, Frances credits her mother, Mary Martha Bond Werner, as her first teacher and mentor.[6]

Mary lived up to her namesakes, the biblical sisters Mary and Martha. Next to the oldest in a family of 12 children – including two sets of male twins – Mary was required to take care of household duties and supervise her younger siblings. Although bright and capable – she earned a certificate qualifying her to attend teachers' college at age 15 – she was prevented by her parents from furthering her education. Girls in the early 20th century often were not seen as needing education beyond homemaking arts, and in adulthood Mrs. Werner often bemoaned her loss: "I wish I could have gone to school!"

"I used to tell her that she was wiser than people with double degrees," Frances said of her mother.[7]

'First by showing, then by doing'

Mary Werner taught her children by example – "first by showing, then by doing," as her middle daughter described it. Their mother taught Frances, her sisters and brother social manners, including dining etiquette, and above all, the practice of kindness and welcome that has become known to contemporary Christians as "the ministry of hospitality."

Mrs. Werner was known far and wide as a wonderful cook and an exceptional baker, turning out mouth-watering bread and desserts from a wood-burning stove. "It was a rare day when some relative or community member didn't arrive at mealtime," Frances recalled.[8]

A typical Thanksgiving menu testified to Mrs. Werner's talent. The feast for the Werners' family and guests included creamy mashed potatoes, baked squash, green beans, Waldorf salad (made with grapes from which Frances had carefully picked out the seeds), relish plates with carrots and celery shining like jewels, lush yeast rolls and freshly churned butter, surrounding huge platters of white and dark turkey meat and bowls of stuffing. Later came a choice of pie with homemade ice cream.

At other times, guests would share in one of Mrs. Werner's delicious meals while they discussed their concerns with Harry and Mary: how best to care for an ailing relative, how to treat a sick farm animal, or whether Harry and his hired hands could help with harvesting or transportation. Those tables of hospitality were blessed by Mrs. Werner's skill as an organic gardener of vegetables and fruits. She also knew much about food preservation, stocking up on homemade canned fruits and vegetables, relishes and pickles plus jams and jellies, to sustain her farm family through harsh Michigan winters.

There were times when an excess of visitors meant setting several extra places at the table, adding more water to the soup, and cutting meats and desserts into smaller portions. Still, no one ever left Harry and Mary Werner's home hungry in body or in soul, and their children took in their parents' example along with their mother's good cooking.

Frances and her siblings especially loved their mother's butter-making, a tasty treat that made up for their tiring hours of turning a wooden barrel churn. "My mother was marvelous at using the wooden butter paddle to mound the butter into molds," said Frances. Stored in the lower compartment of the kitchen icebox, the quart-sized butter crock often bore child-sized hand prints, but "nobody" was the culprit.

The unseen guest

God was always the unseen guest in the Werner household. Meals were preceded by grace, and bedtime by prayers. Sunday was the day everyone went to the Methodist Episcopal Church in LeRoy, where the Werner children attended Sunday school and recited the Bible verses their mother had taught them. More often than not, church dinners centered on mountains of chicken, supplied from Harry's coops and fried to a golden brown in Mary's kitchen.

Just as Mary Bond Werner shone in homemaking and hospitality, Harry Burton Werner became a leader in their farming community, known for his listening ear and his wise solutions to people's problems.

Harry loved conversation, "often forgetting that he had work to do and no money in his pocket," his daughter said.[9] Frances said she learned "Political Science 101" from her father, who had a keen interest in local, state and world affairs. Harry read daily newspapers, and freely gave his opinions on world events. Often, when the political discussions became heated, Mrs. Werner would interject, "I wish you would stop arguing." Harry's standard reply was, "We're just debating."

Although busy with the farm, Harry saw it his duty to serve in community leadership. He chaired the local school board, served as a supervisor for the township of LeRoy, and in later years was elected to the Michigan State Legislature. He often thrilled his children by seating them next to his desk in the legislative chambers to watch the proceedings.

Harry Werner also was a leader in their church. He served as lay leader for many years, and later in life became so involved in church activities that he became known as "Mr. Methodism" throughout the region.

Frances' father was as much a teacher as her mother, but his teaching style was much different. One of his favorite habits was to quiz the children at mealtimes. Frances said she clearly remembers the times her father asked them to solve an arithmetic problem while they were having dinner: "If you have a coal bin, 10 feet by 12 feet, and 8 feet high, how many cubic feet would be available for a load of coal?" By then a sturdy 10-year-old farm girl with a mop of thick auburn hair, Frances said, as she responded with the answer, she thought to herself, "Who cares?"[10]

Work and play

Frances' father was also ahead of his time in believing that his daughters could, and should, learn to farm as well as his son. All the Werner children had daily responsibilities and barn chores. Their help around the farm was greatly needed during the 1930s, when there was no money to hire sufficient extra hands. Kathryn, Frances and Pauline were expected to milks cows, feed animals, tend sheep, drive teams of horses for cultivation and cut corn by hand with a curve-bladed corn knife, just as their brother Forrest did. "When we had cut what our arms could manage, stalks were placed by a slanted wooden saw horse and firmly tied by Dad. He also showed us how to make shocks of grain from bundles of wheat or oats, which the horse-driven binder had cut and tied with binder twine. We would take a tied bundle under each arm, and place them firmly together on the cut stubbles, with the heads of grain together for drying," Frances recalled.

Harvesting potatoes was one of the toughest jobs on the farm. Schools closed for a week of "potato vacation" at harvest time, and aching backs were the norm at the end of the day. Rows of potatoes were dug up, plant by plant, using potato forks, and the harvesters bent over to pick them up. Working as a team, the Werner children moved bushel-sized crates along the rows until the crates were full.

Frances and Forrest frequently were sent to fetch wood for their mother's stove. After they loaded up their little red wagon, they'd test each other's performance going up a small hill towards the house. If Frances was pulling, she'd stop, and so would the loaded wagon. Then she'd tease her brother: "You're not pushing!" And the wily Forrest would reply, "You're not pulling!" Often this debate took so long that their mother would appear, and then the wood would be delivered quickly.

One of Frances' Saturday jobs was to refill the kerosene lanterns and lamps, trim the wicks and wash the glass chimneys. Next came scrubbing the barn creamery room, where the cows' daily output was separated into milk and cream. A local dairy picked up the gallons of cream and turned them into butter and ice cream, which was sold to families in the village of LeRoy.

Another chore for the Werner children was pulling the small red farm wagon to the ice house, where they stored ice that their father and others had collected from nearby frozen lakes in wintertime. Using tongs, they'd pull a block of ice from its sawdust packing, and take it quickly home to cool the pantry's icebox.

Cattle tending

Frances and Forrest often tended the cattle together, chasing them to pasture land a mile away from the barn. As a result, the two middle siblings drew especially close to one another, sharing hopes and dreams and confidences as they drove the cattle to pasture.

"Our parents taught us to be responsible in completing assignments," Frances said. "We did not question their authority and early-on learned to do as we were told."

Living on a farm during the Great Depression taught the Werner children to be creative with their playtime.

They took narrow strips of lath, fashioned a small cross piece on one end, and used them to roll steel rims discarded from wooden wagon wheels. The small farm cart became their wagon to give one another rides. "We learned it was dangerous to ride down the hill in it without a steering gear attachment," Frances recalled. "A few dumps off the road onto the stone pile at the bottom of the hill quickly ended that activity."[11]

Without television, digital video players or other marvels of the Information Age, the Werner children became acute observers of the world around them. One favorite game was to imitate the ways their friends walked, and have others guess the identity of the person from his or her gait. The Werners played tag and hide and seek, and rode horses with neighbor children on Sunday afternoons, while their parents' strictly observed Sabbath time gave them freedom from unnecessary farm chores. In the winter months the children ice-skated together on nearby lakes, and tobogganed and skied down neighborhood hills.

In the summertime, when the corn crib was empty, Harry let his children turn the space into a playhouse. Pauline and Forrest used the front half and Frances took the back portion, because she was a stickler for keeping her play house space tidy, and didn't want her brother and sister tracking through it. Pauline and Forrest generously never kept Frances from passing through their space to get to her area.

Often the children held tea parties, supplied with real treats from their mother's kitchen. One hot summer day Frances made "pretend Kool-Aid" by dipping red crepe paper into water. Forrest went into Frances' play area and, finding the "beverage," drank it. Sometime later, his sister inquired, "What happened to the red liquid?" Forrest confessed, and luckily suffered no ill effects.

Work and play often left Frances and her siblings still keyed up when bedtime came. When the noise grew too loud, Mrs. Werner rapped on the bottom stair with a 12-inch wooden ruler and demanded quiet. The ultimate threat came if the chatter persisted: "Do you want me to have your father come up there?" Their father never had to appear.

Growing in faith

Religion played a central role in Frances Werner's life from birth, as it did in for many in America at the time. Her formative years coincided with two of the 20th century's most significant periods of social, political and economic upheaval: the Great Depression of the 1930s, and the years of World War II and its aftermath in the 1940s.

According to Wessels Living History Farm in York, Nebraska, many farmers borrowed money to buy land or machinery during the 1920s, pledging all their assets to guarantee the loan. Land values and crop prices were high when many of the loans were made, but land values plummeted when the American economy collapsed in 1929. No one had any money to buy land, and so farmers couldn't sell their land to pay off their loans. Banks took back the land to sell it and get back their money.[12]

While the Werner farm was secure, when Harry and Mary were living in Detroit soon after their marriage in 1920, he lost his job at the Ford automotive plant. The loss of his income resulted in foreclosure of some mortgaged city property they had purchased. Many other families were in the same situation. At that time Harry was talked into returning to the farm, as his parents John and Catherine were ready to retire to be near their daughters, Gladys and Sally, who lived in Evart, Michigan. Mary said good-bye to her employer, a medical doctor who needed her to care for his daughter and home during his office hours. He and his daughter regretted Mary's departure.

"People turned to churches, and times of prayer with others in the community, for support, comfort and guidance, while enduring the great economic turmoil and loss of jobs and income," Frances wrote in a personal essay.[13]

One strong Methodist tradition helped shape Frances' girlhood faith: the summertime camp meeting. During the summer months, camp meeting sessions were held at Albright Park in Hersey, Michigan. On Sundays, Mary Werner packed a picnic lunch and the six Werners climbed into their Model T Ford and rode 20 miles through the country-side to camp. After lunch, there was a worship session in the pavilion for the children, with lots of singing, scripture reading and preaching.

The summer when she was eight years old, Frances responded when the preacher invited "anyone wanting to have Jesus come into their heart" to come to the altar. Since the moment she kneeled with others in prayer at that camp meeting, Christ has been a presence in her life, Frances said.[14]

School days

Like many children reared on farms, the Werners attended primary school in a one-room school house from first through eighth grade. Imagine going to school, where your father was on the school board.

Any misbehaving in class was sure to get double correction – first from the teacher, and then at home from Father and Mother!

The school was located a mile from the Werner farm, so there was a daily two-mile trip, walking to and fro to get their education. The walk to school was on top of another two-mile round trip – in the opposite direction — that Frances and Forrest made chasing the cows to and from the pasture during grazing seasons. They did have time to change clothes and have a snack, often freshly baked bread spread with sweet cream and a bit of sugar, before heading for the pasture land. Frequently, when a couple of horses were not being used, they would lead the bridled horse to the farm gate, where they would climb up to mount and ride without saddles.

A highlight of her grammar school years was the summer when Frances was 12. That year she won a trip to 4-H camp in Gaylord, Michigan, by taking first prize for the dress she made in a sewing class.

Frances graduated from grammar school and went on to LeRoy High School. Her four years there culminated in a class trip on the ferry boat across the lake from Ludington to Milwaukee, Wisconsin. Gasoline and tires were still being rationed because of the military needs of World War II. Family photos show the senior class took their excursion as an opportunity to show some grown-up style, complete with jackets and sunglasses.

In 1944, at age 16, Frances Werner graduated third in her class of 15 students, serving as class secretary.

An ambition for nursing

Frances had wanted to be a registered nurse since her childhood, inspired by her mother's example of caring service. But Sparrow Hospital Nursing School required its entrants to be at least 18 years old, meaning that Frances would have to wait until September 1945 to matriculate.

Immediately after graduation, Frances' Aunt Sally Bruce, a beautician with a beauty shop in Evart, Michigan, sought to entice Frances to enroll in beauty school and work in her shop. Sally even had a representative from the beauty school try to recruit Frances. He asked why she wanted to become a nurse, and Frances told him she wanted to help people. "You can help them by working on their appearance," he replied. To this

The Werner family farm near LeRoy, Michigan, where Frances Maxine Werner was born in 1927.

Frances Alguire's parents, Harry B. Werner and Mary Bond Werner, were her first teachers and mentors in life.

10

The Werner family — (front to back), Forrest and Frances, Kathryn and Pauline and parents Harry and Mary Werner — gathered on the steps of their farmhouse for a picture.

At age 12, Frances Werner won a trip to 4-H summer camp as her first-place prize for making this dress for a sewing contest.

Frances Werner and her namesake, maternal grandfather James F. Bond, on their common birth date celebration July 11, 1945.

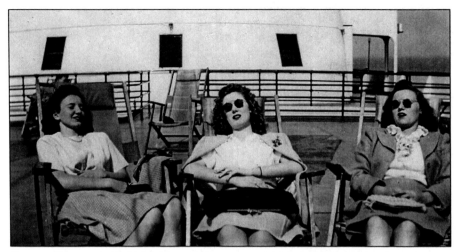

Frances Werner (at left) and her classmates enjoyed their high school graduation trip across Lake Michigan in 1945.

Frances in her graduation picture in 1944 and as a student nurse in 1947.

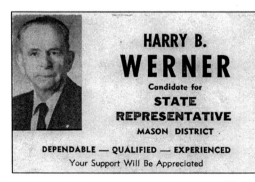

Harry Werner taught Frances "Political Science 101" through his service in the Michigan Legislature and his interest in national and world affairs.

Frances Maxine Werner and Donald Eugene Alguire were married September 10, 1949, in the Methodist Church of LeRoy, Michigan. Their wedding party included (from left), Fran's older sister, bridesmaid Kathryn Zurakowski; Fran's younger sister, maid of honor Pauline Werner; second cousin, flower girl Carol Brehm; the bride and groom; Don's college roommate, best man Vern Swanson; and Fran's brother-in-law, groomsman Bill Zurakowski. Others not pictured were the soloist, Leonora Pamment, Fran's nurses' training roommate, who married Fran's brother Forrest Werner, one of the two ushers, about four months later. The other usher, Don's friend Karl Aven, married Fran's sister Pauline one year later.

Early in their marriage, Donald and Frances Alguire frequently welcomed her father, Harry B. Werner, to their rented rooms in Lansing, Michigan, when Mr. Werner would arrive for sessions of the Michigan Legislature.

statement Frances responded primly, "No, thank you."

Instead, Harry and Mary Werner arranged for their second daughter to stay with her older sister Kathryn in Wyandotte, Michigan, while her husband Bill Zurakowski, was serving as a second lieutenant in Germany for his second year of duty. Later Frances reflected she wasn't sure whether her parents sent her to keep her sister Kathryn company, or to separate Frances from her high school boyfriend.

Kathryn and Bill were married in 1943 after graduating from college. Kathryn was employed as a chemist with Sharples Chemical Company in Wyandotte.[15]

Frances left LeRoy on her first Greyhound Bus ride, arriving in Detroit where Kathryn met her. The sisters took local transit to Kathryn's apartment in Wyandotte.

At age 17, Frances needed to get a work permit in order to get a job. Once she had her permit in hand, she started walking through Wyandotte's business section, stopping wherever she saw a "Help Wanted" sign.

Working at the deli

She was hired at The Pure Food Market on Biddle Street on her first morning out. The market's owner, Jack Kaplan, gave Frances an orientation on working in the deli and meat department, overseen by butcher Sam Randazzo and his sisters, Rose and Mary.

Meat was being rationed in 1944 while World War II was still under way. Red-colored ration stamps were required for customers to buy meat. Sometimes small wild game such as rabbit and muskrat was available for purchase without ration stamps.

Frances and her co-workers cut ox tails between the small bones and tied them together for customers to use in making soup. Day-old lunch meat and end-pieces too small for slicing were ground up with pickle relish and a little mayonnaise to be sold as "ham salad." The "ham salad" was a favorite sandwich spread for many customers.

Occasionally, Jack would come by to check on his staff as they weighed meat products. In the days before digital scales displayed weights visible to customers, the market owner was pleased if Frances and her co-workers "accidentally" read off an extra ounce or two for a customer's order. When the boss wasn't around, the customer benefited.[16]

The Pure Food Market was open until 9 p.m. on Fridays and until 8 p.m. on Saturdays. The schedule meant that Frances walked 11 blocks home to their apartment in the dark. "My protection was a long hat pin easily available from the side of my purse," she said. "My siblings still tease me about this, but fortunately I never had to put it to the test."

Frances' year in Wyandotte was an education in more ways than one.

Kathryn had majored in home economics in college, and she taught Frances much about food preparation and sewing. They visited the amusement park, theaters and parks in and around Detroit. With the war still on, there were many sailors on shore leave who stopped to talk with the attractive sisters.

Frances went home to LeRoy for Thanksgiving and another of her mother's bountiful holiday feasts. When Christmas came to Wyandotte, her employer Jack Kaplan gave all his employees a bottle of wine. As a faithfully abstaining Methodist, Frances told her boss that she didn't drink alcohol. So instead of wine, he presented her with a ten-dollar bill!

The year in Wyandotte passed quickly. Before she knew it, World War II was officially over, her brother-in-law Bill came home to her sister Kathryn, and Frances was back in LeRoy, preparing to enter Sparrow Nursing School.

A student nurse

Frances recalled that it was a sunny, colorful "Indian summer" – her favorite time of year – when Harry and Mary Werner drove their daughter 200 miles to Sparrow Hospital Nurses' residence in Lansing, Michigan. This was the time she had anxiously awaited, yet their parting was a tearful good-bye. Frances was on her own for the first time, without family members to surround her.

The nurses' residence was a three-story brick building with several offices, a formal lounge, large auditorium and classrooms, a small kitchenette with snacks and a laundry room on the first floor. Frances, whose high school class had been 15 students, soon discovered she would have 53 classmates.

New students were assigned to the second floor, in single or double rooms with bunk beds. Upper classmates lived on the third floor. Frances was given a single room but during her three years there had two different roommates, including one who later married her brother. Each day began at 7 a.m. with devotions, followed by class lectures and study time. Days and evenings were spent pouring over textbooks in anatomy, psychology, chemistry, pharmacology and nursing arts. Two years of Latin had been required for entrance into nursing school. When it came time to prepare case study reports, however, Frances said her need was for typing skills.

Among their "professional preparation" texts was a book, "Twelve Tests of Character," by Harry Emerson Fosdick, one of the pre-eminent preachers of his day and author of the hymn, "God of Grace and God of Glory," still part of The United Methodist Hymnal.[17]

Fosdick's exhortations must have sounded to Frances like her parents' teachings:

> *"To care about the welfare of mankind supremely, to rejoice in better work than ours which helps the cause along, to be interested in the thing that needs to be done and to be careless who gets the credit for doing it, to be glad of any chance to help, and glad, too, of any greater chance that another may possess, such magnanimity is both good sense and good Christianity."* [18]

Frances and several of her classmates were U.S. Cadet Nurses, which meant that their uniforms were furnished, along with tuition, board and books and a monthly stipend of $15. They earned additional income by caring for doctors' children. As Cadet nurses they agreed to serve for the duration of the war.

Upended in a wreck

One evening as a doctor was driving Frances home from her baby-sitting job at his home, his car was sideswiped and flipped over, landing on the driver's side with the motor still running. Quick-thinking Frances suggested that the doctor turn off his engine to avoid an explosion.

The doctor was in a state of shock at the wreck, but Frances escaped with a bruise on her upper arm. The police called a taxi for her so she could return to the nurses' residence before her 11 o'clock curfew. When Frances reported the incident to her house mother, however, the house mother insisted that Frances go to the emergency room for a check-up.

Her car accident was a shock, but that fright paled in comparison to the students' nursing arts instructor, Miss Thompson, who was a stern taskmistress, to put it politely. She cast such an exacting eye over the students' bed-making that some of them actually trembled when she asked, "What did you do wrong?" Frances said later, "We learned not to take extra, unnecessary steps as we tightened sheets and made square corners for the covers."

One of the "tricks of the trade" that the student nurses had to master under Miss Thompson's scrutiny was sterilizing a thermometer.

Unlike the 21st century's digital read-out thermometers with disposable plastic covers, thermometers were long, thin glass tubes containing mercury when Frances Werner went to nursing school. They were sterilized between uses by placing them in a jar of isopropyl alcohol, and were considered contaminated if they touched the glass above the alcohol when being removed. Frances and her classmates tried not to smile when a telltale "ting-a-ling" revealed that some nervous student's thermometer hadn't made the proper exit.

One day, one of Frances' classmates, a young woman named Celia, was learning to perform a colon irrigation. Miss Thompson asked Celia: "What direction does water flow?" Instead of raising the irrigation container and replying "down," Celia considered the direction she was facing and answered, "East."

'The best nurses'

Years later, Celia, Frances and their classmates still laughed over that episode at reunions. When Miss Thompson, at age 90, attended their 50th class reunion, Frances confided that she and her classmates had been afraid of their formidable instructor. Miss Thompson smiled as she replied, "I wanted you to be the best nurses."

Six months after they began their training, the probationary students received their caps and became real freshmen. By that time, nearly half the class had either failed or decided nursing was not for them. Frances was not among the drop-outs, a feat in itself.

Now the students' classroom lectures were extended, as doctors began to instruct the nurses on their respective specialties. Even more attention was paid to the formation of the young women's characters. Miss Ganger, their director of nursing, admonished her charges to "never wear black patent leather shoes, as they reflect up, and never sit on a boy's lap unless there is a newspaper between you." These comments generated great hilarity after the student nurses congregated on the second floor, Frances recalled.

Clad in white uniforms with white shoes and stockings, their hair off their collars or in a net under their caps, the nursing students began their first experience with patients during the time known as "PM care." This late-day duty, after visiting hours ceased at 4 o'clock, involved taking patients' vital signs — temperature, pulse and respiration. The student nurses gave out warm wash cloths so patients could freshen their hands and faces, rubbed sore backs to ease muscles cramped from hours in bed, and poured fresh drinking water.

Going about these tasks, Frances had no inkling that before long, she'd be a patient herself.

A slide into mishap

During their second year of training, Frances and her friends Celia and Shirley often went out together. One warm summer evening, they walked to nearby Potter Park. The playground area, with its swings and slide, were inviting to young women still in their teens. They took turns going down the slide.

"In those days, we wore starched cotton dirndl skirts, very slick on the surface," Frances recalled. "I got going too fast."[19] Sailing off the slide, Frances landed hard on her tailbone. "Something was wrong," she recalled. "My middle went numb. I felt like my body could be lifted apart through the middle."[20]

With darkness approaching, Frances sent her friends to get help, not thinking what she'd do alone if threatened by a stray dog or other animal. She was concerned for their safety as young women if one was seen walking alone at night. Celia and Shirley found an available telephone near the park entrance, and called the nurses' residence, where Miss Ganger answered. When she offered to collect them in her car, Frances' friends told her to send an ambulance, because Frances had sustained a back injury.

At the hospital, X-rays showed Frances had suffered a compression fracture of the 12th thoracic vertebra. By now it was midnight, and Miss Ganger wanted to telephone Harry and Mary Werner about Frances' injury. Frances demurred, asking her nursing director to wait until morning.

It was noon the next day before Miss Ganger telephoned the Werners, confiding that Frances hadn't wanted her parents to know about her injury. Mary Werner was shocked when she arrived later that day to find Frances in traction. Frances told her worried mother, "I requested Miss Ganger to wait until morning to notify you. I knew there was nothing you could do last evening except lose sleep."

~ "During the weeks of traction I learned a great deal about being a patient," Frances wrote later.[21]

After weeks in the hospital, Frances was immobilized in a body cast and sent home to rest for three months. She thought her nursing career might be over. Then as now, nurses had to be of rugged health to deal with their patients' needs, and a broken back might prove a disqualifying injury.

However, when the body cast was removed, her doctors fitted Frances for a back brace, and she thankfully returned to nursing school. She was assigned three months in the diet kitchen for her required time there, then night duty in obstetrics, where there was no lifting, and the next three months in the formula room, where nursery bottles and nipple tops were cleaned and sterilized and filled with freshly made formula. The body brace Frances wore each day gave her spine the necessary support. After nine months she was healed sufficiently to manage without the added support.

The accident put Frances three months behind her class at nursing school. Though behind on her studies, she was allowed to remain with her senior class. That was how, on March 5, 1948, Frances ended up with her classmate Shirley in an office of the nurses' residence, preparing name tags for the men from Michigan State College coming to the monthly dance party. Among the first to arrive was a young chemical engineering student named Donald Alguire.

Two little words

The dance at the nurses' residence bore the theme of "March Whirl." The name tags being made up by Frances and her classmate were in the shape of miniature kites.

Frances printed "DON" on one of the little kites, but her guest protested. "Nobody can read that." She quickly answered: "I can." Frances said later, "Little did I know what a lasting impression those two little words had made."[23]

Don asked Frances for the first dance. Then came a mixer and they were separated. Don sought out Frances for the third dance and asked if she would join him and a friend at a movie. She demurred, because her class was in charge of the dance. So Don promised absolutely to have her back in time for clean-up.

Soon they were on their way by city bus to see "Voice of the Turtle," arriving back in time to meet the midnight Saturday curfew and assist with clean-up.

Before they parted, Don asked Frances for a date on the following Saturday evening. She accepted, but then during the week, her work schedule was changed to the 3-to-11 shift at Sparrow Hospital. She called to cancel their date because she had to work, but Don thought he was getting a brush-off. That's when Don exhibited a perseverance that he'd become known for later in life. He asked Frances for another date, and she accepted.

During the next six months, Don and Frances regularly enjoyed one another's company. Frances was allowed to go through the graduation ceremony with her nursing school class later that spring, even though she didn't finish her studies until summer. Then came cramming for two days of state board examinations at Wayne State University in Detroit for her nursing license.

By fall 1948, Frances was serving as nursing supervisor of a medical and surgical floor at the Lansing city hospital. Don had two more years of study to complete his degree in chemical engineering. But that didn't stop him from asking to place an engagement ring on Frances' finger.

'You didn't ask me'

Flushed with excitement, the two young lovers made the trip back to LeRoy and the Werner family farm to inform Frances' parents of their engagement. Upon learning the news, Harry Werner looked at Don and said, "You didn't ask me if you could get married." "We were never sure if he was joking or not," Don said, but he replied, "I knew if your permission was needed she would have told me."

At first Don wanted to wait two years to marry, so that he could finish school and find a job to support his wife. But Frances was working and paying rent, and Don was paying room and board at Michigan State. They soon decided it made better sense to marry sooner and share the cost of living.

So on a beautiful Saturday afternoon. September 10, 1949, Frances Maxine Werner married Donald Eugene Alguire at the little country Methodist Church in LeRoy, Michigan, surrounded by family, friends and classmates.

Frances' and Don's good fortune in finding one another apparently rubbed off on their well-wishers that day. Six months later their soloist, Leonora (Lee) Pamment, married Frances' beloved brother, Forrest Werner, and one of Don's groomsmen, Karl Aven, married Frances' younger sister, Pauline, the following September.

Married life

Frances and Don went to Niagara Falls, New York, on their honeymoon trip. They returned to a two-room apartment on the east side of Lansing originally rented by Frances and her sister Pauline, who attended Acme Business School in Lansing. Pauline and one of her classmates had located a new residence before the wedding.

The Alguires' first home was on the second floor, accessed by an open stairway outside. The trip downstairs to work and college turned treacherous if rain, ice or snow had fallen overnight. The apartment had a small kitchen with a tiny table and two chairs. Their bedroom was another small room with a sofa bed, across an open hall that also led to the bedrooms of the landlord's children.

Unfortunately, the only bathroom in the house was off that hall, between the Alguires' two rented rooms. Every time the landlord's preschool-age son Jimmy heard Frances or Don go into the bathroom, he climbed up the stairs and began a dance outside the door, with a sense of urgency.

Frances walked eleven blocks to her job at the Lansing hospital. Meanwhile, Don walked out about three blocks, then hitchhiked five or six miles to get to his classes at Michigan State. When the young couple needed groceries, Don met Frances at the hospital, then they walked together to a nearby grocery store, and returned to their apartment carrying their grocery bags.

One of the highlights of their first home became the weekly visits of Frances' father.

Harry Werner was serving in the Michigan House of Representatives, which met in Lansing from Monday evening until Friday at noon. Harry had his own room near the capitol building, but he always stopped on Mondays to have supper with Frances and Don. Naturally, he brought food from the farm, including, butter, Mary Werner's homemade bread, her canned fruit and vegetables and fresh garden produce.

Often Don accompanied his father-in-law to the legislature's Monday night sessions, Don sat next to Harry in a guest chair on the House floor to observe the proceedings and be introduced to other legislators..

Sometimes Harry had Frances and Don deliver him to his rooming house, then loaned them his car. The first time they took Harry's car, Don drove Frances to work. Thinking the road to the hospital was a main thoroughfare for which cross-street traffic had to stop, Don was shocked when a car pulled in front of Harry's car – and legally had the right-of-way.

The result of Don's misunderstanding didn't enhance the looks of Harry's car fender.

"Bless my dad, he paid the minimum charge that his car insurance didn't cover, and he and Don stayed the best of friends," Frances recalled.[24]

Chapter 2
'That Talented Lady'

One evening in 1957, Donald Alguire, chair of a committee to start a new congregation, and his vice chairman, Dr. Ted Jackson, were sitting in the family room of the Alguires' home in Battle Creek, Michigan. They were discussing how to start a new congregation on land that Dr. Jackson and Dr. Roberts, both veterinarians, had donated for a Methodist Church in the midst of a developing subdivision.

Every so often, Don's wife, Frances, would chime in on the conversation while she was preparing dinner. After about 30 minutes or so of this room-to-room conversation, Dr. Jackson turned to Don with an insight: "Don, you are not the top Methodist in this room. It's that talented lady getting your supper. Remember my words in your future."[1]

The Alguires had little inkling at that point how right their guest was. The training ground for Frances Alguire's leadership as the world's "top Methodist" came in local congregations, and through the Methodist Woman's Society of Christian Service, now known as United Methodist Women.

An idyllic era

Frances and Donald Alguire were a young married couple, with two preschool-age daughters, when they began in earnest to serve in leadership with the Methodist Church, a predecessor denomination of today's United Methodist Church. The arc of their lives, especially the development of Frances Alguire's leadership skills during this period, reflected an era in American life that seems distant and idyllic from the perspective of the early 21st century.

Frances was then what today is called a "stay-at-home" mother. Most women did not work outside the home, so it was considered entirely normal for Frances, although a registered nurse, to devote herself to making a home for her family and rearing their two daughters, Mary and Catherine.

As it was for most of America in the 1950s and early 1960s, Frances and her women friends and neighbors were available during the day to socialize with each other while their children played, and to provide leadership and support for church and community activities. The tremendous growth of the Methodist Church during this period can be attributed not only to the influx of the "Baby Boom" generation that included Mary and Catherine Alguire, but to the hard work and dedication of their mothers, millions of unsung church women. While only a few visionary people such as Dr. Ted Jackson realized it at the time, during this era Methodist women such as Frances Alguire were learning managerial and leadership skills through homemaking that they would later translate to a wider world.

The Alguires joined First Methodist Church of Battle Creek shortly after they moved there in 19523. Before long, Fran was leading one of the Young Mothers' circles of the Methodist Woman's Society of Christian Service, and both she and Don were serving on church committees.

In the early fall of 1954, the church asked the Alguires to represent First Methodist at the Methodist Family Life Conference in Cleveland, Ohio. Fran and Don left their daughters Mary, barely three, and Cathy, still an infant, with their aunt and uncle, Kathryn and Bill Zurakowski — the first time Mom and Dad had left their little girls with someone else. The Alguires were impressed by the many excellent speakers and panel presentations, along with the scriptural address by host Bishop G. Hazen Werner. The plan was for Don and Fran to report on the conference at their church's family night supper, some Sunday evening in early November.

'Never speak in front of a crowd again'

The Alguire family had moved to Battle Creek because Don accepted a position with the Post Cereals Division of General Foods. The Thursday before the Alguires were to give their report to the church, Don's employer offered him a position as Analytical Research Supervisor, and he was told, " the job might entail some travel."

After discussing the offer with Fran that Thursday night, Don accepted the new position on Friday morning. By Friday afternoon, Don was told to prepare to be on an airplane to Dallas, Texas, the following Sunday afternoon.

Frances dressed in her Sunday best, put on her hat, and prepared Mary and Catherine for their time in the church nursery. She ended up giving their report on the Family Life Conference by herself — the first time she had ever spoken before a large crowd..

She told Don afterward that she would "never speak in front of a crowd again."[2]

That first trip was the beginning of a lifetime of business-related travel for Don Alguire. By 1958, he was away on business several days out of every month. "Fran kidded at our 40th wedding anniversary that we had been very happily married 40 years and lived together 26 years," Don said.[3]

Don's professional travels had a direct effect on his and his wife's ability to encounter new situations and manage stresses and frustrations that would thwart less-experienced people. Soon, Frances and the girls looked forward to spring break from school and time to travel with Dad, as well as during the summer season. On long auto trips they would combine vacation with Don's business and enjoy camping out in route. "We have fond memories of overnights in several national parks as we enjoyed the scenery and time with other campers," Frances recalled.

The more often Don traveled, the more Frances gained in "on-the-job" management training, since she usually remained at home with their daughters.

A budget in envelopes

Don and Fran set up a family budget by putting various amounts of money in separate envelopes for house payment, utilities, insurance, food, charity, and so on. Of course, if something unexpected came up, some money would be "borrowed" from another envelope.

Once, early in their new situation, Don had just left home on another business trip when the water heater broke and flooded the basement. Frances got her first taste of dealing with a major household appliance repair — and negotiating with a repairman.

Despite the young family's tight budget, the Alguires put an increasing percentage of their money aside for the Lord. Each time Don received a raise, the percentage of their income given to the church increased, until they reached the level of a biblical 10 percent tithe. Over the ensuing decades, their contributions — in "prayers, presence, gifts and service," as the current United Methodist membership vow states — would grow far beyond the biblical minimum.[5]

By 1956, Don was serving on the Greater Battle Creek Methodist

Union, a body that functioned to coordinate activities of the city's Methodist churches. He was tapped to chair a committee, which he had to form himself, to decide what to do with a $20,000 bequest left to the churches belonging to the union.

The first meeting of the committee was held in the recreation room of the Alguires' home. Before the meeting was over, the group had transformed itself into a new church founding committee. Several names for the church were suggested, but because the land that Dr. Jackson and Dr. Roberts had donated was on a small rise, the committee finally decided to name it Chapel Hill Methodist Church.

Frances was chosen to organize Chapel Hill's Woman's Society of Christian Service, while Don led the new congregation as lay leader. While Chapel Hill was being developed, the Alguires also housed two seminary students, who did the field work of canvassing the neighborhood and surrounding area in preparation for starting the new congregation. The fledgling church had the benefit of the Alguires' leadership for only one year before they moved again.

Moving out of Michigan

In 1958, Don took a job as Midwest Technical Service Manager for the Borden Company's Special Products Division, headquartered in Elgin, Illinois. As Frances described the move:

"It was a cold February day in 1958 when the moving van took our possessions to another state. Our Werner family is a caring, loving family. I felt sad about moving from my native state and all my relatives to the Chicago area. We had located a small rental house in South Elgin. Daughter Mary was enrolled in first grade and Don was busy with his new job. This left pre-school daughter Catherine and me to do the unpacking and amuse ourselves in this small community.

"My homemaking duties in this rental house became routine and quickly accomplished. We were a one-car family back then. After a few weeks of exploring the community with Don on the weekends, I knew that I could drive him to his office and participate in community activities during his working hours and find my way home."[6]

Elgin had five Methodist Churches when the Alguires moved there. They decided to join the 1,200-member First Methodist Church down-

26

town and "get lost in the congregation," as Fran put it,[7] feeling the need for a sabbatical after their hectic stint leading the start of Chapel Hill Methodist Church in Battle Creek, Michigan.

For a few weeks, the Alguire family had the blissful experience of being part of the crowd. They worshiped as a family on Sundays, attended Sunday school classes, and participated in couples club events. Then Frances decided to attend the monthly Woman's Society of Christian Service luncheon meeting and was happy to find a nursery provided for preschoolers.

'Embarrassed to be singled out'

"The first meeting I attended, I entered the dining room where others were already seated," Frances recalled.[8] "The senior minister, the Rev. Dr. Carlton Rogers, saw me and immediately rose and tapped on his water glass for attention. He said, 'Ladies, I want you to meet Mrs. Alguire. The Alguires are new members transferring from Battle Creek, Michigan, where they were both leading committees for a new church.' I felt embarrassed to have arrived a few minutes late and then to be singled out."

The next week, Mrs. Alguire was contacted by the Nominating Committee of the Woman's Society of Christian Service. She was asked to serve as the Chair of Spiritual Growth. "I thanked them for thinking of me, but I declined," Frances said.

A few days later a knock at the door announced a visit from Dr. Rogers. After a cordial chat, Dr. Rogers said he was acting on behalf of the WSCS Nominating Committee. "He was a very persuasive person," Frances said. "He told me if I waited until I was acquainted we might be moving. I ended up saying 'yes' to being nominated."

Like Ted Jackson, Carlton Rogers saw something beneath the demure manner of the petite, auburn-haired Mrs. Alguire, and he pressed her into service. In her first year in Elgin, Frances gave two talks on spiritual life for the churchwomen, and was asked to present ten-minute devotionals on the local radio station each week during Lent.

From that point on, Frances Alguire began speaking in church quite a lot — especially for someone who vowed she'd never again speak in front of an assembly.

During their four years in Elgin, Frances and Donald Alguire both became active in many church and community activities. Frances said they felt guided by some familiar verses from Book of Proverbs:

"Trust in the Lord with all your heart, and do not rely on your own insight.
"In all your ways acknowledge him, and he will make straight your paths."
— Proverbs 3: 5-6 NRSV [9]

The Alguires purchased an older, two-story home on Commonwealth Avenue within walking distance of Wing Park, which provided a community pool, playground, picnic areas and a nine-hole golf course. Daughters Mary and Catherine learned to swim, and Don joined a golf league.

Don was president of the Elgin chapter of Young Republicans, a task in which his wife helped. Meanwhile, Frances quickly became acquainted with dozens of Methodist women in Elgin by participating in WSCS activities. As Spiritual Life Chair at First Methodist, she was responsible for planning and presenting worship services, devotionals and Bible study. Her own spiritual practice deepened as she prepared to lead other women.

Ever-present faith

"Mom's strong belief in God, the Creator, the Empowerer, the Guider, the Protector, was ever present in our upbringing," wrote her daughter Catherine Alguire in a remembrance.[10] "She held steadfastly to her beliefs and convictions and put forth daily effort into practicing them as well as making sure that we, her children, also knew these tenets. She was a nurse by training and by nature — in the professional sense and as the verb is defined, always wanting to make others feel better and reminding us that 'it is better to give than receive.' "

Catherine Alguire said that her mother continued to feel a "strong and passionate" identification with her nursing profession even after she and Don had children. "We certainly benefited from her caring and 'nursing' nature. We were the children with the mother who would always bake cookies for the sales, make special things for our classes, encourage us to participate in new things and sew us lovely clothes, sometimes even with matching outfits for our dolls. Being ill as a child was a always mixed blessing — in spite of how awful one felt, Mom always found the few things that were appetizing and brought them to us to eat in bed. And likely, they were served on a fancy tray with special napkin and a flower. Usually the combination of the appreciation for, and the guilt of getting, this unanticipated luxury of gourmet bed service would make me get better, get up and get going."

Searchers' inspiration

Soon after the Alguires settled into the Elgin home, Frances was invited to join The Searchers Club, a community Women's Club, centering on "elegant monthly luncheons and interesting programs," as she recalled. While many of the club members were also Methodist women, her new membership further expanded her network of church and community relationships. She found inspiration in the Searchers' Club motto:

> *Attempt the end and never stand to doubt*
> *Nothing so hard but search will find it out.*[11]

In addition to WSCS and Searchers, Frances became an active member of her daughters' Highland School PTA, a Brownie Girl Scout leader, a director of the Young Women's Christian Association, secretary of the local women's political club, and a participant in monthly meetings of a church circle.

"During these four years, I learned a great deal from the many women I served with, as well as from the leadership and ministry of Dr. Carleton Rogers," she recalled.

Once, after she led devotions at a church event, Dr. Rogers said to Frances, "Someday you will be president of the world Methodist organization." Forty-eight years later, Frances recalled, "I had no idea what he was talking about at the time, but his prophetic words had been planted. He saw something in me that I never saw in myself."

Dr. Rogers died in 1996, but he lived long enough to see his prediction come true, as that summer Frances was elected president of the World Methodist Council during its meeting in Rio de Janeiro, Brazil.

If any two words could sum up Frances Alguire's life between 1960 and 1996 when she moved into the top echelon of World Methodist Council leadership, those two words would be "travel" and "energy."

In 1962, Don accepted a new position with Griffith Laboratories Co., a food ingredient manufacturer, to develop a new business for them in "contract" food product sterilization. Dr. Lloyd Hall, Griffith's retired Research Director, held over 60 patents and one was for the elimination of bacteria and mold on dry food ingredients using a dry, low temperature gaseous ethylene oxide for treatment.

Because of Fran's previous work as Supervisor of Sparrow Hospital's Central Supply Department, Don recognized that a new process was needed to sterilize the plastic disposables and medical equipment then making their way into the market, since plastics wouldn't hold up to the old-fashioned steam sterilization methods of sterilization. So Don, as a graduate chemical engineer, was aware that plastics could be sterilized using ethylene oxide. He promoted the contract sterilization possibility to all the major medical manufacturers. His inspiration eventually led Griffith Labs to create a subsidiary company, Griffith Micro Science, in 1970. In 1999 Donald Alguire's vision was borne out, when Griffith Laboratories Co. sold the subsidiary to a Belgian company for $165 million.[11]

'The girls were concerned'

With the new job came another relocation. This time the Alguire family moved into a three-bedroom, brick ranch-style home south of Hinsdale, Illinois, a southwestern suburb of Chicago. Mary enrolled in fifth grade, and Catherine in third grade. Each morning, Frances watched her daughters as they walked a short distance to wait for the school bus.

"The girls were concerned about what I would do home alone all day without them," their mother said.

Frances' and Don's daughters, Mary and Catherine Alguire, recalled that, as if to relieve their misgivings, their mother threw herself whole-heartedly into her roles as homemaker, hostess, volunteer, mother and wife. In the language of the late 20th and early 21st centuries, Frances became a mistress of multi-tasking.

"As a result of her strong work ethic and drive to excel, Mom had high standards for herself and others," Catherine wrote in a remembrance.[12] She took the responsibility to learn the skills for which the situation called, and assumed that by her model, others would do likewise," Catherine recalled. "As a homemaker, she refined her already-honed cleaning and gardening skills, as well as excelled in home decorating and culinary skills. I honestly don't remember a single time during my child-

30

hood that I ever saw our dining room table not decorated, a bed not made or dirt anywhere in the house.

"As the wife of a business executive, Mom became well known for her exceptional hostess abilities, creating wonderful dinner parties and making all kinds of wonderful foods. She provided these same elaborate meals for family, always with dessert and reminders of healthy nutrition. Once she became involved in volunteer work and needed to attend many long meetings, she became talented in sewing, needlework, and several other kinds of handwork, meaning that she not only excelled in the professional arena but created wonderful handmade gifts for family and friends. As young adults, my sister Mary and I once joked that with all the lavish attention Mom gave us, perhaps she needed more than two children — and perhaps, she felt this too, so she invested her energies more fully in her church family."

Automobile adventure

With the move to Hinsdale, Don became a Burlington railway commuter, taking the train into Chicago each day for work. As a typical suburban family of the early 1960s, the Alguires owned one automobile, which meant that Frances drove Don to the station each morning at 6:30 and returned for him in the evening.

"Often I would drive the short distance in my bathrobe," Frances recalled.[13]

Frances' and Don's past adventures with automobiles — Fran's accident in the doctor's car and Don's mishap with side-street traffic — held true for their commuting era as well.

One early morning, in an era about 20 years before cellular telephones became popular, just as Don boarded the train, the car engine began steaming and sputtered to a stop.

"Fortunately I found a dime in the glove compartment [to use a pay telephone] and called a nearby service station," Frances said. The trouble turned out to be a broken water hose, which the service station attendant quickly repaired. Frances was home from her auto adventure before the girls awoke for school.

While settling into their new community, the Alguires learned that a new congregation of Methodists in Hinsdale had been chartered recently. They met Sunday mornings in the village community center, arranging furniture for a worship space and Sunday school classes. "Shades of *deja vu*," Frances wrote in a remembrance, "that was where we had left the Battle Creek congregation four years ago: meeting in temporary facilities!"[14]

The Alguires discovered the ministry of the founding pastor, the Rev. Dale Nelson, to be "spiritually stimulating." They joined the fledgling congregation and within a few months attended the groundbreaking of Hinsdale Methodist Church.

Making new friends

In April 1962, Frances and Don met Vivian and Bob Miner, who lived in nearby Clarendon Hills, Illinois. They were also visitors at Hinsdale Methodist Church. The meeting produced a friendship that has lasted nearly 50 years, and gave the new church a capable team to lead its Woman's Society of Christian Mission.

In 1963, Frances Alguire was elected president of the Hinsdale Methodist Church's Women's Society of Christian Service. With her are officers (from left) Reta Schwisow, Peggy Binfield and Rosalie Herzog.

As Vivian Miner tells it: "We connected right away. . . . Soon after we first met, we discovered that Fran and I are one day apart in age and both raised on a farm, hers near LeRoy, Michigan and mine near Leroy, Wisconsin. She and I have occasionally reflected on our 'farm girl heritage.' We think it had much to do with who we are: industrious, committed, humble, thankful, tolerant and appreciative."

Soon Frances and Vivian were attending the new Woman's Society of Christian Service monthly meetings together. Within the year, Frances was elected president and Vivian was elected vice president for two-year terms.

"Obviously, her gift of Christian leadership was recognized early," said Vivian. "She's organized and well-prepared. She inspires others to lead by her example, undergirding them with confidence. She always takes Christian mission seriously and as a part of her daily living. She combines mission with the joy of working with others. She has a wonderfully positive, 'it can be done' attitude, laced with cheerfulness and humor.

"Above all, her humility exemplifies itself [as being in partnership] 'with,' never [leading from] 'above,' " Vivian said in her recollections of the time.[15]

"Being part of a new church, there was need for many fund-raising projects," Frances recalled. "Several very capable members participated in preparing church dinners. We had book reviews, style shows, antique and rummage sales and bazaars, all to raise money for missions and the needs of our new church. These were busy times but great friendships evolved as we worked and prayed together."[16]

Busy and productive

During Frances Alguire's term as president of the Hinsdale Methodist Women, she represented the church regularly at district and annual conference events: annual meetings, leadership training sessions, conference schools of Christian Mission. At the same time, Pastor Dale Nelson taught Bible study each Tuesday morning and Frances was a regular participant.

The Woman's Society of Christian Service met monthly as well as the small group sub-units known as "circles." Church activities, school events and PTA meetings along with rearing her two daughters and homemaking duties kept Frances busy, but even her leisure time was productive. In the evenings, for relaxation while Don was on business trips, the former 4-H Club sewing contest winner stitched dresses for her girls and even pieced a quilt.

Frances' 1963 date book shows the year began with several parties with church friends and neighbors. Along with Vivian and Bob Miner, the Alguires remain friends with Rosalie and Barney Ill, Bob and Doris Pharo, and Rita Schwisow from Hinsdale Methodist Church.

Business duties required Don to spend three days from the first full week of January in Washington D.C., and the third week Frances, Mary and Catherine were alone again while he was in New York City and Union, New

Mary Alguire explores a Halloween Jack jack-o'lantern while waiting for her new baby sister and mother to come home from the hospital.

Catherine and Mary often wore "sister" dresses. They were great playmates.

Mary and Catherine Alguire as young women.

Frances and her daughters Mary (left) and Catherine in 1976.

PRESIDENTS OF THREE UMC ORGANI-ZATIONS FOR WOMEN - pictured at a recent mission team meeting for United Methodist Women of NIC are Frances Alguire (Mrs. Donald) newly-elected first President of United Methodist Women; Rowena Aldrich (Mrs. Arthur), first president of the Woman's Society of Christian Service from 1941-45 (which came into being with the merger of the former Methodist Episcopal Church; Methodist Episcopal Church, South; and the Methodist Protestant Church in 1939 to form the then Methodist Church) and Norma Wieting (Mrs. Wesley) first and only president of the Women's Society of Christian Service (1969-73). The change from Woman's to Women's came about upon the 1968 merger of the former Evangelical United Brethren and former Methodist Churches into the United Methodist Church.

A newspaper clipping from 1974 tells the story of transition for The United Methodist Church.

Mary Bond Werner marks her 80th birthday with her children (from left), Kathryn, Pauline, Forrest and Frances.

Jersey. Frances soon learned the route to O'Hare Airport from Hinsdale.

"Often the weather was stormy, and traffic was such that policemen would not allow you to linger by arrival areas," she recalled. "Being 'pre cell phone era' sometimes making connections and correct timing were difficult. Our daughters were too young to be sent to the baggage area to wait for Daddy while I stayed with the auto."[17]

Coping with the unexpected

Frances said that Don often returned home from his busy week exhausted, bearing a heavy briefcase full of notes and ideas to be sorted and compiled into a report for Monday morning. "He carried his attaché case almost constantly. It's no wonder after all these years his left shoulder joint is often sore," Frances wrote sympathetically in a remembrance.

Don enjoyed the challenges from his new job and his many associates. Frances met new neighbors, and parents of her daughters' new friends. Her duties as mother and homemaker allowed time for church and community activities.

By March 1963, her date book showed a typical week for Frances Alguire looked like this:[18]

Sunday	Church 11:00 a.m.; 6:15 p.m. take Don to airport.
Monday	10:00 a.m. Committee meeting at Wiley's
Tuesday	9:30 a.m. Bible study; 2 p.m. dentist
Wednesday	Brownie Scout leaders meeting
Thursday	4:15 p.m. Take girls to church choir rehearsal
	7:00 p.m. Cathy piano practice;
	8:00 p.m. Committee Meeting.
Friday	6:15 p.m. Meet Don's plane from Newark.
Saturday	10:00 a.m. Mary to confirmation class
	1:00 p.m. Cathy piano recital

These activities from Frances' calendar were in addition to cooking, cleaning, shopping, laundry and caring for the girls and their needs. Frances was also the family's social secretary, making phone calls, writing letters and keeping up with friends and out of state family members.

"There were occasions when the washing machine didn't function, the furnace broke, and the car needed servicing that interrupted routine and taught me to cope with the unexpected," Frances wrote in a remembrance.

Along with Don's new job as National Sales Manager for one area of Griffith Laboratories (in fact, he was the only salesperson in this area of their business at the time) and the trips his position entailed, the Alguires continued serving on church committees. They found their service both a benefit to the church and a way to get acquainted with the community. They made frequent trips to museums, theaters, and special programs.

One way Frances and her daughters coped with Don's extended absences was to take advantage of the cultural wonders of Chicago. They made frequent trips to museums, theaters, and special programs. "There were months when we felt like city tour guides as we showed the sights to our frequent visitors," Frances said.

Following in Dad's footsteps

In 1966, two years after their move to Hinsdale, Frances took another step away from her resistance to speaking in front of groups.

First, she agreed to serve as a lay member of the Northern Illinois Annual Conference from Hinsdale Methodist. She was spurred to her new participation in part by the death earlier that year of her devoted father, Harry Werner, "Mr. Methodism" of central Michigan.

"I remembered that serving at annual conference was something my father used to do," Frances said.[19]

Second, her two-year term as president of the Woman's Society of Christian Service at Hinsdale (1963-65) had brought her to the attention of Northern Illinois Methodist women. She accepted in early 1966 the nomination to be Chicago Western District WSCS President. Later at a Northern Illinois Annual Conference session, the resident Bishop Paul Washburn told her, "Fran, I'm seating you with the district superintendents so those from the EUB and Methodist traditions can get to know each other and work together more amicably."[20]

The family's calendars and Fran's daybook for the years 1966 through 1970 show a whirlwind of activity. While social and political revolution swirled around America, the Alguires anchored themselves in the traditional values and activities that had long shaped their lives.

There were Sunday school classes and worship each Sunday at Hinsdale Methodist. There were monthly meetings of the Women's Society of Christian Service, often with Fran leading devotions, and the annual conference-wide society meeting. There was the Woman's

Society's annual School of Christian Mission, a practice that continues to this day under the sponsorship of United Methodist Women. Frances also faithfully attended meetings of the conference committee on Methodist Social Concerns.

Interspersed with church meetings during this period were social gatherings such as the monthly dinner-bridge night for the Alguires' neighborhood, political meetings like the Republican Women's Club for Fran and the Young Republicans for Don, work with the Hinsdale South High School Boosters' Club and serving as an adult chaperone at the Hinsdale Youth Center. In 1969, Fran and Don had a taste of "high life" when they were invited to attend the inaugural ball of the successful Republican candidate for Illinois governor, Richard B. Ogilvie. [21]

In short, their lives were as rich and full as anyone could have hoped, and no one in the Alguire family at that time could have imagined what God yet had in store for Frances and Donald.

Inspiration and innovation

Fran's continued service with the Methodist Woman's Society of Christian Service had made her a major asset to the Northern Illinois Annual Conference. She also was gaining more experience in the ways of politics by helping Don, who had become a Republican precinct committeeman and a member of the party's Downers Grove Township and DuPage County Board. By the time Don chaired the party's township board in 1970 and 1971, even daughters Mary and Cathy had learned to help in political campaigns.

There were also plenty of family and household management tasks to stretch Fran's skills. Don was still traveling about two weeks out of every month. The Micro Biotrol Co. subsidiary of Griffith Laboratories was growing so fast because of Don's work in expanding medical product sterilization and other products, such as food and cosmetic powders, that it seemed he was constantly selling his bosses on building another plant somewhere in the United States or around the world. What started out as three small facilities eventually became 17 stand-alone plants around the world, whose managers all reported to Donald Alguire. [22]

In 1968 the family took a dream vacation — 21 days in Europe, covering eight countries. Fran and Don took with them their teen-age daughters Mary and Catherine and Fran's mother, Mary Bond Werner. It was the first time Mrs. Werner flew in an airplane. "We wanted to have this experience as a family before the girls left us for college," Fran said.

"We thought at the time, 'This may be the only time we ever get to Europe,' " Don wrote in a memoir.[23]

The Alguires' professional, community and church work began to involve them in expanding circles of responsibility and influence as the decade of the 1970s began, in much the same way that the 1968 merger of the Methodist Church with the Evangelical United Brethren Church had expanded the scope of the new denomination, The United Methodist Church.

In mid-1971, Don talked Griffith into buying a radiation sterilization company in Dickerson, Maryland. With the new company came a responsibility to attend and help run a sales booth at the 4th World Conference on the Peaceful Use of Atomic Energy, held that year in Geneva, Switzerland.

The Alguires had just moved into a new home in Downers Grove, Illinois, a countryside area, and had two daughters in college, but they managed to get Catherine off to Mary Washington College in Fredericksburg, Virginia, and Mary off to Vassar College in Poughkeepsie, New York, for her junior year. Fran and Don flew to Geneva, Switzerland, with fond memories of their family's visit there in 1968.

Celebrating the new

After its first General Conference as a newly formed denomination in 1972, The United Methodist Church began the hard work of adapting its structure and mission to its new identity. The former Woman's Society of Christian Service of the Methodist Church joined with the former Wesleyan Service Guild of the Evangelical United Brethren Church to form United Methodist Women.

In October, 1973, 130 women from Northern Illinois Annual Conference traveled by bus and auto to the National Assembly meeting of United Methodist Women meeting in Cincinnati, Ohio. The theme "Many Gifts, One Spirit" was designed to help the women of the newly formed denomination build community and share in exciting possibilities for a new future together.[24]

In January, 1974, the conference newspaper reported that Frances

Alguire had been elected the first Northern Illinois conference president of United Methodist Women. One of her first acts was to pay homage to one of her predecessors, Rowena Aldrich, who had served as the first president of the Woman's Society of Christian Service from 1941 to 1945, following the three-way merger of the northern and southern branches of Methodism with the Methodist Protestant Church to create the Methodist Church in 1939. In a letter dated February 27, 1974, Mrs. Aldrich expressed her appreciation to Frances for continuing to include her:

Dear Fran:

Yesterday I receive a copy of the [report from] the Northern Illinois Conference Mission Team meeting held Jan. 12 at Naperville. I sat down right away to read it, for I am always deeply interested in what is going on in the conference. . . . Much to my amazement, I found that in the new organization I am still being kept on as Honorary Life Member of the Mission Team. I cannot express to you how my heart was warmed by this decision, for I had surely felt that now it would be an entirely "new ball game" and because so many of the officers are new (at least to me) they would surely see no reason for any exceptions being made.

I do not know for sure, but I can guess that you, Fran, were responsible for this honor, and I do so much appreciate it.

. . . Now I am 81 years old — long past retirement time — but my interest in the work has never waned. And I do want to keep in touch with the wonderful work you are doing as long as I can. I know I cannot attend night meetings, for while I still drive a good deal, my family do not want me to drive any real distance at night and I'm sure I should not do so. However I will attend any day meetings possible, and where I can't [attend] you will know my heart is with you.

I have not known you very many years, but from the first time I met you and knew a bit about you I felt you were a very special person, and as the years have gone by, my opinion has increased manyfold. I am so happy that it is you leading our women in the big task which is yours to do.

May God's richest blessings be upon you every hour of every day . . .   Rowena Aldrich

Some of the issues involved learning a new mission statement and new titles for familiar offices and programs. Each local congregation's UMW chapter became a "unit," rather than a "society" or a "guild" as in the past. Some of the adjustments reflected the new sensitivities of the growing women's movement.

For instance, Frances recalled, "How to list names in the directory was debated — whether to list the husband's name [as was the social custom at the time] or the woman's given name. Some felt strongly about each option. A compromise was reached, with the decision to list the given name with that of the husband in parenthesis, where appropriate."[25]

After social niceties, a bigger, more politically charged challenge loomed for United Methodist Women in the effort to ratify the Equal Rights Amendment to the U.S. Constitution, which was approved by the Congress in 1974.

A struggle for equal rights

On its face, the Equal Rights Amendment was one of the simplest additions ever proposed to the U.S. compact of a democratic republic, according to "The History Behind the Equal Rights Amendment" by Roberta W. Francis, Education Chair, ERA Task Force, National Council of Women's Organizations.[26] Here is its entire text:

THE EQUAL RIGHTS AMENDMENT

Section 1. Equality of rights under the law shall not be denied or abridged by the United States or by any state on account of sex.

Section 2. The Congress shall have the power to enforce, by appropriate legislation, the provisions of this article.

Section 3. This amendment shall take effect two years after the date of ratification.

Dr. Francis wrote further:

"The Equal Rights Amendment passed the U.S. Senate and then the House of Representatives, and on March 22, 1972, the proposed 27th Amendment to the Constitution was sent to the states for ratification. But as it had done for every amendment since the 18th (Prohibition), with the exception of the 19th Amendment, Congress placed a seven-year deadline on the ratification process. This time limit was placed not in the words of the ERA itself, but in the proposing clause.

". . . Like the 19th Amendment before it, the ERA barreled out of Congress, getting 22 of the necessary 38 state ratifications in the first year. But the pace slowed as opposition began to organize — only eight ratifications in 1973, three in 1974, one in 1975, and none in 1976.

"Arguments by ERA opponents such as Phyllis Schlafly, right-wing leader of the Eagle Forum/STOP ERA, played on the same fears that had generated female opposition to woman suffrage. Anti-ERA organizers claimed that the ERA would deny woman's right to be supported by her husband, privacy rights would be overturned, women would be sent into combat, and abortion rights and homosexual marriages would be upheld. Opponents surfaced from other traditional sectors as well. States'-rights advocates said the ERA was a federal power grab, and business interests such as the insurance industry opposed a measure they believed would cost them money. Opposition to the ERA was also organized by fundamentalist religious groups."[27]

United Methodist Women had voted to work for ratification of the ERA, upholding the tradition of equal rights for women that had been fostered by their Methodist women ancestors of the 19th century. Despite this history, however, there were male and female United Methodists who, like those cited by Roberta Francis, had serious reservations about what the amendment would mean for American society.

In the Northern Illinois Conference, President Alguire asked Margaret Wilkins to serve as conference coordinator for promoting the amendment. Ms. Wilkins worked tirelessly in trying to dispel myths related to the issue. The effort in Illinois suffered a serious setback, however, when the state legislature changed its rules to require a three-fifths majority to ratify an amendment. This change ensured that Illinois state legislators' repeated simple-majority votes in favor of the ERA did not count toward ratification.[29]

'Not an act, but an action'

The first birthday of Northern Illinois United Methodist Women was celebrated on November 9, 1974 at Court Street United Methodist Church in Rockford. Theme for the day was "Christianity . . . Not An Act But Action." A birthday candle had been prepared by conference Vice President Shirley Seaman, who collected used candles from each local unit, melted them and molded the blended wax into one large candle that was kept lighted throughout the program.[30]

United Methodist Women of the Northern Illinois Conference took the "action" part of their birthday theme seriously. That year the conference's offering for missions went 4.4 percent over its pledge, with $412,532.26 given by United Methodist Women. At the close of the birthday celebration, Frances Alguire was surrounded by balloons containing each woman's gift statements. After the colorful flying toys were gathered, members popped the balloons, sharing aloud with one another their promises of increased giving of time and money, being more hospitable, inviting new members, attending School of Christian Mission, and many other charitable works.

The new calendar year began in January 1975 with a two-day retreat of conference leaders for planning and goal-setting. That year the Northern Illinois Conference tested six proposed programs for the churchwide UMW Program Resource Book being prepared by the Women's Division. The units' evaluations were tabulated by conference leaders and reported to the Women's Division. One program written by conference member Beth Bishop was included in the new book. Because of her talent and insight, Beth Bishop was elected Northern Illinois Conference UMW president to succeed Frances Alguire, when Fran was elected to the Women's Division Board of Directors in 1976.

Devoted to making life better

Then as now, United Methodist Women are devoted to making life better for others. Locally Northern Illinois UMW units supported Bargains Unlimited, a resale store on Clark Street in Chicago, by supplying good-quality resale items and volunteering help with display and sales. Proceeds from Bargains Unlimited supported Marcy-Newberry Mission Centers. Meanwhile, the sale of Esther Hall House in Chicago, formerly a residences for women immigrants and refugees, had provided funds for more missions. Northern Illinois UMW leaders decided to establish a revolving fund for the needs of the Marcy-Newberry Association; $10,000 for a Grant-Loan Fund for women pursuing education in church-related vocations; and a "love gift" for the emerging needs of the Women's Division, the administrative arm of United

Methodist Women.

Conference UMW Vice President Shirley Seamon was appointed by President Frances Alguire to represent United Methodist Women, along with members of the conference Board of Laity, in planning for an annual retreat to which all women of the church would be invited. Vice President Shirley was also named liaison for United Methodist Women with the newly formed Commission of Status and Role of Women, a conference committee relating to the new denominational agency, the General Commission on the Status and Role of Women.

Headed to General Conference

The 1975 annual session for Northern Illinois Conference was held in June that year at the Northern Illinois University in DeKalb. Bishop Paul Washburn requested Frances, attending the conference as the United Methodist Women's representative, to give the benediction following the opening night banquet. She and her husband Don were seated a the head table with Bishop Paul and Mrs. Kathryn Washburn and other program participants, bringing her leadership skills again to the forefront.

Delegates to General and Jurisdictional Conferences were to be elected at the 1975 session, and United Methodist Women were well-organized for the campaign. Promotional slates of hopeful candidates were circulated. Margaret Wilkins, the conference UMW representative on the Equal Rights Amendment, prepared badges for women leaders with their ballot number boldly displayed in big letters. As a result of the women's hard work, Frances Alguire, a laywoman, was the first person elected to the 1976 General Conference from Northern Illinois.

Frances' service with the 1976 General Conference, the first time she was chosen for the denomination's highest legislative assembly, marked her biggest step yet in leadership. She was also elected to chair the Northern Illinois delegation with the Rev. Dr. Edsel A. Ammons, then a professor at Garrett-Evangelical Theological Seminary in Evanston, Illinois, as vice chairperson.

The United Methodist Church, including the historically progressive Northern Illinois Conference, was still getting used to the idea of women and laity in leadership when Frances was chosen to chair the 1976 General Conference delegation from her conference. Among her first innovations was to break the tradition of seating the delegation with clergy in front and laity behind. Frances organized the seating so that laity and clergy delegates were placed alternately beside one another in the order of their election. This practice has since become common through United Methodist annual conferences, but it was a major innovation in 1976.[31]

Once every four years

The United Methodist General Conference occurs once every four years. It is composed of no more than 1,000 representatives, elected from each annual conference, each Central Conference (regions of the church outside the United States) and from "concordat churches," other Methodist bodies with whom The United Methodist Church has a formal sharing agreement, such as the Methodist Church of Great Britain. General Conference is the only body with the authority to speak for the entire denomination. Its primary task is to enact the provisions of United Methodism's two ruling documents, the Book of Discipline, the enduring collection of church policy, and the Book of Resolutions, a set of guidelines on timely topics.

The Book of Discipline is the oldest continuous document of church policy and law in the Methodist movement. Most churches of the Wesleyan tradition base their operations on their own Book of Discipline. For The United Methodist Church, the Discipline includes the constitution of the church; its "theological task" and doctrinal statements; the Social Principles, a collection of United Methodist policies on political, social, scientific and other issues; and most importantly, a set of commonly agreed standards by which the church will operate, organized into sections called "paragraphs."

While each General Conference can vary, the assembly typically has ten or eleven legislative committees assigned to survey a different section of the Book of Discipline and consider proposals for changing the church's stances and standards. Delegates are assigned to reviewed hundreds of petitions having to do with the local church, the ordained ministry, the general boards and agencies, the Social Principles, the superintendency and so on.

In other words, The United Methodist Church, through its General

Conference, has the opportunity to remake itself completely every four years, according to the delegates' discernment of God's will for the church in a particular time. Thus delegates to General Conference bear a heavy responsibility. In the year prior to General Conference, delegates spent hundreds of hours reading the Discipline and comparing its existing policies and practices with petitions seeking change.

Many meetings

Frances Alguire led many meetings with the Northern Illinois delegation about legislative committees and resolutions from the Advance edition of "The Daily Christian Advocate," the official journal of the General Conference. In addition, she was often asked to speak to local groups about issues to be acted on at General Conference. Often she was more of a listener at these sessions as people shared what they were against. For the 1976 General Conference, issues that drew stiff opposition included gender-inclusive language in liturgy and the Holy Bible, the Equal Rights Amendment, and human sexuality. Frances learned to listen carefully to the impassioned comments — sometimes fueled by misinformation — of concerned clergy and laypeople. In the end, Frances frequently reminded her audiences that there would be 1,000 persons from United Methodist conferences and Concordat Churches debating, discussing and amending all proposals before final votes would be taken. Whatever their views, their membership and ordination vows formed a covenant among United Methodists to live with the results of the 1976 General Conference, as codified in the Book of Discipline and the Book of Resolutions.

Between General Conference sessions, the programmatic work enacted by delegates is assigned to The United Methodist Church's general boards and agencies. These bodies are composed of elected directors who decide policy, supervise and approve budgets and nominate the agencies' top executives, known as general secretaries, who at the time were confirmed by the church coordinating body known as the Council of Ministries. Directors of boards and agencies serve a four-year term and are elected at each Jurisdictional Conference following the General Conference. There are five jurisdictions in the United States: Northeastern, North Central, Southeastern, South Central and Western. The Northern Illinois

Annual Conference, which Frances Alguire represented in 1976, is part of the North Central Jurisdiction, composed of the United Methodist regional units in the states of Illinois, Indiana, Iowa, Michigan, Minnesota, Ohio, North Dakota, South Dakota and Wisconsin.

Electing bishops

Jurisdictional Conferences in the United States are all held during the same week, typically in July, for another primary purpose: the election of the church's "general superintendents" known as bishops. Clergymen — and in 1976 the candidates for bishop were still all men — were proposed from each annual conference within the Jurisdiction and interviewed by delegates during the jurisdictional meeting. The number of bishops elected each four years is determined by the number of bishops who are retiring and the number of episcopal areas needing an executive. Episcopal areas may have one or more annual conferences, but typically not more than three, because of the demands of supervision, especially travel.

Unlike lay people such as Frances Alguire, whose church membership resides in their local congregation, the membership of ordained clergy is in their annual conference. Once a clergyperson is elected a bishop, his or her membership moves to the Council of Bishops, the global body of United Methodist general superintendents. So while election to the position of bishop is the highest honor The United Methodist Church can bestow upon its ordained clergy, it is also one of the most difficult, fraught with long hours, hard work, much travel and the sacrifice of one's life in a local setting to be a leader of the global church. Becoming a bishop requires the deepest spiritual preparation, along with more human skills of administration and the ability to teach, which is one of a bishop's primary tasks for the church.

At the 1976 North Central Jurisdiction Conference held in July in Sioux Falls, South Dakota, the Rev. Dr. Edsel A. Ammons, who served with Frances Alguire in leading the Northern Illinois delegation to General Conference, was elected bishop along with Rev. Leroy C. Hodapp.

Unlike her brother in Christ, Edsel, Frances was not called to sacrifice her local community. Yet she, too, was chosen at that meeting for church-wide leadership. Frances was elected to a four-year term as a director of the Women's Division, which also meant that she served as a director of the United Methodist General Board of Global Ministries. Bishop Paul Washburn also appointed Frances and Donald to be lay members of the World Methodist Council, meeting that August in Dublin, Ireland. Frances also attended the World Federation of Methodist Women's meeting held in Dublin prior to the World Methodist Conference.

The transition to Frances' new responsibilities was daunting. After the World Methodist Council meeting in Ireland, she flew to New York City in September for orientation and organization of Women's Division and Global Ministries directors. Fortunately during the World Federation of methodist Women's meeting, Frances had made a new friend, Dollie Christ from Tequesta, Florida, who proved to be an invaluable mentor for Frances as a first-time director.

New assignments

Dollie had been elected to her second four-year term as a Women's Division director. While they were together in Dublin, Dollie asked Frances to be her roommate when they attended Women's Division and United Methodist Board of Global Ministries meetings. They continued to share a room whenever they attended board meetings together for the next four years. Dollie knew the Women's Division staff and introduced Frances to many new directors. Dollie also shared what to expect during meetings and guided Frances to where certain offices were located in the church's headquarters at 475 Riverside Drive in New York City. Although assigned to different Women's Division committees, the two roommates made time to get together and exchange information from their experiences.

Frances was assigned to the Women's Division Section of Christian Social Relations, to the Finance Committee and appointed chairperson of the Committee of Development Education. For Global Ministries, she was assigned to the Division of Christian and Interreligious Concerns. This division later became the General Commission on Christian Unity and Interreligious Concerns.

During September, Frances also continued to attend meetings of the Northern Illinois conference Board of Missions, Council on Ministries, and participated in the Women's Division Section of Christian Social

Relations meeting at O'Hare Airport. She spent four days in October at Silver Lake, New York, attending the Women' Division Finance Workshop, then went back to Illinois for the conference missions banquet in Elgin. Mid-October Frances traveled to Denver, Colorado, for her first annual meeting of boards of Global Ministries and Women's Division. Downers Grove UMC requested her as the speaker at its three Sunday morning services on the last Sunday of October.

Since the Women's Division prohibited a woman from serving in two positions of United Methodist Women at the same time, Frances was required to relinquish her position as president of Northern Illinois United Methodist Women.

Frances' last two major official acts were significant. On September 6, 1976, she participated in organizing the 400th unit of United Methodist Women in the Northern Illinois Conference at Friendship United Methodist Church in Bolingbrook. Six weeks later, at her last conference meeting on October 27, 1976, she saw the fruits of her emphasis on inviting young women into UMW membership, when more than 100 women under the age of 39 were present. In a sign of passing their responsibility to a new generation, women residents of the Wesley Willows retirement community in Rockford, Illinois, each presented a corsage they had made to the under-39 members.[32]

At the end of the year, Frances turned over her considerable files and duties as conference UMW president to Beth Bishop. The Northern Illinois United Methodist Women's 1976 Directory quoted its outgoing president:

"We are grateful to God for the many dedicated leaders, of the past and present, throughout the Northern Illinois Conference, who have helped us move 'Beyond A Dream' into Christian global responsibility and service. United Methodist Women are called to serve everywhere. What will be your special calling and area of service during this 'historic' [American] Bicentennial Year?"[33]

Frances Alguire's special calling had taken her into the age of worldwide service to Methodism.

Chapter 3

'Local Woman - Change Agent'

The June 1977 issue of *Response*, the magazine of United Methodist Women, featured an essay by first-term Women's Division director Frances M. Alguire. The article was titled "Local Woman - Change Agent."

WHAT NEEDS CHANGING?

Recently I had lunch with five United Methodist Women I knew well, and have worked with closely on several occasions at district and local levels. I posed the question: "If you saw an article titled, "Local Woman - Change Agent," what would you expect to read?

The first woman to remark questioned, "What needs changing?" This spontaneous remark relates the attitude United Methodist Women have toward changes needed. There was no hesitancy or feeling of helplessness, but instead an interest to respond where needed.

United Methodist Women have many resources available to help them with their personal or programming development. Some are a variety of printed material, Schools of Christian Missions, Leadership Training Sessions, conference and district events, plus help from jurisdictional and national leaders and staff.

We went on to discuss problems and needs of persons in our communities — moral decay, drug abuse, crime, broken family relationships, problems encountered by singles and divorcees, housing and counseling needed for runaway teen-agers, poverty, lonely senior citizens, to name a few issues. Each woman present had ideas for solutions or examples of personal participation in these concerns. We sensed that working corporately more could be accomplished. At no time was the comment made: "Things can't be changed." Rather, we realized many problems are complex and need our combined efforts and skills.

As local women we are called to serve in a variety of ways. In *The Shalom Woman*, Margaret Wold states: "Whether it be in global or local concerns, women must begin to see themselves as agents of change. The potential of women as creative innovators is unlimited, if they ever catch on to their own creative ability. Women have incredible amounts of work energy and management ability, a fact that is evidenced in every women's organization and in every volunteer activity they undertake."

These women lunching together were not without special concerns in their own lives. Our hostess had recently undergone a double mastectomy for cancer. Her faith has not wavered, her attitude remains positive, and instead of complaining she is busy with church activities and helping others with their needs.

". . . There are varieties of gifts but the same Spirit. There are varieties of service by the same Lord. There are many forms of work, but all of them, are the work of the same God. In each of us the Spirit is manifested in one particular way, for some useful purpose." (I Cor. 12:4-6 NEB). How do you respond as an agent of change?[1]

In Frances Alguire's case, her election as a director of the Women's Division and the General Board of Global Ministries, coupled with her initial experience as a delegate to the World Methodist Council, elevated an active "local woman" to a "change agent" on a global scale.

United, but in transition

Frances Alguire's collaborative leadership style and organizational skills were greatly needed by The United Methodist Church at the time she was chosen for churchwide service. Formed in 1968 by the merger of The Evangelical United Brethren Church and The Methodist Church, the new United Methodist denomination had weathered nine rocky years of changes, but more lay still ahead.

In 1977 the United Methodist Church had about 9.5 million members in the United States, with several thousand members in Europe, Asia and Africa.[2] Church leaders had been working through two General

Conferences to craft a new denomination that balanced the traditions of its heritage with the realities of its new existence. While the Evangelical United Brethren, or EUB, tradition and the Methodist tradition converged in many ways, there were also strands that were unique to each branch.

One EUB tradition was that of a central program coordinating group, which the new denomination embodied in its General Council on Ministries. The Council was composed of representatives from each general agency, along with directors assigned specifically to the Council. Its responsibilities included coordination of the denomination's budget in cooperation with the General Council on Finance and Administration; conducting research on the state of the church and its ministries; and final approval of the chief executives, known as general secretaries, of all boards and agencies.

Another major challenge for the denomination was the incorporation, from the Methodist Church, of churches and clergy from the racially segregated Central Jurisdiction. The Central Jurisdiction was created as a compromise in 1939 to ensure the participation of the Methodist Episcopal Church, South in a three-way merger when the Methodist Episcopal Church and the Methodist Protestant Church merged to form The Methodist Church. After the Civil Rights Era of the 1950s and 1960s, the Central Jurisdiction was abolished in the 1968 merger of The Methodist Church and The Evangelical United Brethren Church that formed The United Methodist Church. Even into the mid-1970s — in fact, well into the 1990s — United Methodist bishops found it difficult to appoint black pastors to white churches, and vice versa. The issue of race had so profound an effect on the denomination that one of the first new agencies formed was the General Commission on Religion and Race. The commission's first general secretary was the Rev. Woodie W. White, later elected a bishop, who was one of several activist clergy, such as the Revs. James Lawson of Los Angeles, Cecil Williams of San Francisco, and Joseph Lowery of Atlanta, who had been pressing the church for racial inclusion.

Women's status

A third major challenge for The United Methodist Church at this time — and one with which Frances Alguire was familiar — was the status of women in both church and society. Within the church this meant a constant struggle to include clergywomen and lay women in both representation and leadership in the denomination, even though women had gained full clergy rights nearly 20 years earlier. In society, women across America and around the world faced poor health, poverty, degradation and discrimination.. These were concerns that had long had the attention of Methodist and EUB church women, now banded together as United Methodist Women.

Even for someone as active as she was, the new round of responsibilities that Frances Alguire undertook in January 1977 proved a challenge of time and energy.

Frances handed over the presidency of Northern Illinois Conference United Methodist Women to Beth Bishop in December, 1976, but she didn't hand over her membership. If anything, her "citizenship" in The United Methodist Church now stretched her from the familiar activities of Hinsdale UMC to centers of social and political power such as Washington D.C. and New York City.

A whirlwind of meetings

As a director of the Women's Division, Frances continued to meet with conference leaders and in mid-January attended the Northern Illinois UMW retreat. She maintained her activities in local UMW with unit and circle meetings, along with serving on Hinsdale's Council on Ministries. She also had been asked to serve on the Northern Illinois Conference Council on Ministries Executive Committee, which meant a Burlington train ride into Chicago on Jan. 17, 1977.[3]

February 1977 began with Frances speaking at a Lenten breakfast in the Chicago Southern District church at Hazel Crest UMC. Then she traveled to New York City Feb. 6 to 8 for the Women's Division Finance Committee meeting, then back to Illinois for the Conference Council on Ministries retreat Feb. 11-12. Then she flew back to New York for a two-day planning session for the Committee on Social Relations, followed by two days of meetings with Jurisdictional Regional School Committees. She returned to Illinois on Feb. 21 in time to travel to Naperville, Illinois, where directors of the Center For Parish Development were meeting. Frances then flew to Mexico where she met

Don for a six-day vacation in Cozumel. She returned from Mexico in time to attend a planning session at Faith UMC in Chicago for the annual Northern Illinois School of Christian Mission.

In early March, Frances was introduced to The United Methodist Church's efforts to influence U.S. government policy. She joined other United Methodists in Washington, D.C., to meet U.S. Representatives and Senators and discuss issues related to the United Methodist Social Principles. Her first experience of Capitol Hill advocacy left Frances frustrated.

In a conversation with Bishop James S. Thomas, she vented her feelings at realizing that some politicians were more interested in being re-elected than voting what was best for the citizens. A wise and patient Christian leader who counseled many clergy and laity in his time, Bishop Thomas was one of the last bishops elected in the Central Jurisdiction in 1964, and became one of the first episcopal leaders to build bridges between white and black United Methodists. Although at times Bishop Thomas was criticized by his more activist brethren of failing to push more strongly for racial inclusion,[4] his calm spirit and keen intellect poured healing oil over many troubled waters in the early days of The United Methodist Church.

As they walked past a construction site, Frances recalled, Bishop Thomas called attention to a nearby pile of rubble. "It's like that pile of construction rubble," the bishop told Frances. "In time, something good will rise above it." In those few simple words, Frances said, Bishop Thomas gave her an eternal truth that she maintained through years whenever she felt impatient with the slow progress of change.[5]

Broadening horizons

Coming home from Washington, Frances attended monthly local church and conference committee responsibilities, including the UMC Board of Laity Retreat for Women at Williams Bay, Wisconsin. Then another brief respite came in late March through early April, when she accompanied Don on a business trip to England, Belgium, Holland, France and Spain. While Don saw to the needs of his business, Frances used the opportunity to broaden her horizons, visiting friends and touring each country to learn more of its traditions.

Despite Fran's and Don's packed schedules, the Alguires were able to visit their Michigan relatives the end of 1977 for Christmas and New Year holidays. They were delighted that Frances' mother, Mary Werner, agreed to return with them to their countryside home in Downers Grove for a visit in early 1978.

Mary Bond Werner, who had long lamented her lack of formal education, had nonetheless made an active and influential life for herself. Fran's mother had been a member for many years in the Woman's Society of Christian Service and Osceola County Home Economics Club in LeRoy, Michigan. Mrs. Werner also had been an avid supporter of her husband's political activities until his death in 1964.

Catherine Alguire later reflected on her grandmother's influence on her mother. "I know that my mom was close to both her parents, but as my grandfather died when I was young, I was most aware that my grandmother was a strong role model for my mother. My mother revered her and they maintained a very close relationship, in spite of letter-writing being their main source of communication at that time. Mom wrote a letter to her every week, and when Grandma's weekly letter arrived, she would read it out loud to us. She reminded us that Grandma was always busy doing something and that the only time Grandma sat without working was when she was reading or had guests. And even then, she would limit reading time so as not to neglect work or be perceived of as being lazy, and when having company she would remain attentive to the needs of others, getting up to serve them as needed. The inference was that 'idle hands are the devil's workshop,' except that I can't recall Mom ever saying the word 'devil' so she wouldn't actually say that phrase — but we understood."[6]

'You're working too hard'

With this kind of background, it must have brought Frances up short when Mrs. Werner became concerned about Frances' many meetings during her January visit. She told her daughter firmly, "You're working too hard." Despite their close relationship, Frances replied to her mother that she "would have plenty of time to rest when she was six feet under." With her innate wisdom, Mrs. Werner had put her finger on one of the dangers of church leadership: burnout.

Fortunately, Mrs. Werner and her son-in-law Don were fond of each other, so they got along well while Frances attended a two-day meeting for the North Central Jurisdiction meeting in Minneapolis Jan. 20 and 21, 1978. The next day, Sunday, Jan. 22, Frances preached a sermon, "A Great Crowd of Witnesses," at the Glen Ellyn UMC. Later that day she met with Black Methodists for Church Renewal in Chicago. On Jan. 31 Frances took her mother to an ecumenical luncheon. Table groups were all asked to discuss the biblical verse, "Seek ye first the kingdom of heaven" (Matthew 6:33, KJV). The verse generated much conversation, in which Mrs. Werner delightedly took part.[7]

Mrs. Werner's visit concluded the weekend of Feb. 11, when Frances' sisters Pauline and Kathryn and their husbands came for a visit. The families belatedly celebrated the Feb. 8 birthdays of Kathryn and Pauline, then Mrs. Werner returned to Michigan to spend a few weeks with each of her other daughters.

March began with Frances serving as school nurse in Hinsdale, then another round of meetings commenced. March 4 and 5, she was in Albion, Michigan, meeting with Women's Division staff and North Central Jurisdictional leaders for regional School of Christian Mission planning. March 8 she flew to New York City for a week at the Women's Division-sponsored Economic Justice Seminar.

Marathon of meetings

In April came the semi-annual, week-long marathon of Women's Division and General Board of Global Ministries Board meetings. Activities often began with 7 a.m. breakfast meetings, plenary sessions and committee meetings throughout the day, and evening sessions concluding about 10 p.m. By the time Frances and her roommate Dollie Christ had time to debrief with each other about their day's experience, there was little time before midnight to read, sort and reassemble papers for the next day's session.[8]

The work didn't stop when Frances returned home; she just swapped files. After completing her Women's Division/GBGM follow-up, she pulled out her notes on the Northern Illinois Conference Episcopal Committee meeting. The Episcopal Committee functioned somewhat like a Staff-Parish Relations Committee in the local church. The committee works with the resident bishop on any issues related to his or her tenure.

By this time, Frances' activities were earning amazement around the Northern Illinois Annual Conference. She said she was often asked by less active people how she could keep up with all her many activities. She replied that what she learned from participating and listening to others in each group was applicable in many other areas. For instance, Frances had learned organizational and administrative skills during the time she served as supervisor of a medical-surgical floor at Sparrow Hospital in Lansing, Michigan, in the early 1950s. Those skills had transferred to her effective management of the Alguire household for decades, which in turn gave her abilities that she adapted to her church work, and vice versa. She also made use of information she had gleaned from a time management seminar held by the Women's Division staff at one of the Board meetings.

That year Women's Division National Assembly was held in late April in Louisville, Kentucky. Frances hosted a luncheon group where the topic was "The Ethics of Organ Transplants." She had recently seen a New York City stage play, "Whose Life Is It, Anyway?" about a quadriplegic who lobbies for the right to have life-sustaining equipment removed. Among other highlights of this assembly was the presence of Frances' daughters, Mary, coming from Poughkeepsie, New York, and Catherine, coming from Boston.

'I have to vote my conscience'

June 1978 brought the annual session of the Northern Illinois Conference in De Kalb. Since Hinsdale UMC now had a staff with two ordained clergy, it was entitled to two lay members as well, and Donald and Frances Alguire were chosen to represent their church.

In those days before computerized ballots, votes at annual conference were tallied by having members stand. The Alguires were seated together and when votes were called, they occasionally stood to vote oppositely. Members seated nearby became aware of Don and Fran voting opposite one another. In another vestige of the old nemesis, sexism, some conference members commented to Fran that she must have a strong marriage to vote differently from her husband. Schooled by her Women's Division participation, which had given her different insights on some issues, she replied: "I have to vote my conscience."

Sometimes Frances tried to deflect the remarks with humor: "The reason Don is such a good salesman is because we can discuss ideas openly and he knows I will share my thoughts just as I appreciate his." When the comments continued, however, Frances and Don decided they'd sit at different tables at future annual conferences, just to keep the church "gossip mill" from imagining that their opposite votes meant they had marital problems.[9]

Frances' conscience brought her to another event in June, the Midwest Regional School of Christian Mission June 18-23 in Albion, Michigan. In addition to attending classes she led a 90-minute plenary session on the topic, "Racism — Special Emphasis." "Throughout the church there was still much work to be done emphasizing the need to be inclusive," Frances wrote in a memoir. "Saying 'persons of color weren't qualified' was not acceptable." She also used her time in Albion to remind participants that elected directors of churchwide boards and agencies are limited to serving a maximum of two consecutive terms, so part of their mission is to train potential successors. Frances' talks proved interesting enough that she always faced a long line of participants with questions or comments after her presentations.

Frances' leadership on racial inclusiveness continued in late July and early August at the Northern Illinois Conference School of Christian Mission. Her topic this time was the Women's Division-sponsored Racial Justice Charter, in which UMW units pledged to work for racial equality in both church and society. Part of her seminar included suggested ways to present the charter at their UMW programs.

Strong social bonds

Late summer in 1978 was a time for Frances to take a short breather from church work. Instead she served the kind of "ministry of hospitality" that her mother Mary Werner had modeled throughout Frances' life.

In early August Frances supported Don at the annual meeting of his company, now named Micro Biotrol. She provided for entertainment, side trips, and luncheons for the spouses while their mates were in subcommittee. Don and Fran also arranged for the area managers and their spouses to join them for dinner in the evenings. These gatherings included sales personnel from across the USA, Canada and Mexico. Later in August Fran and Don enjoyed picnics with church friends and neighbors and a visit from Don's brother Sam and wife Nancy.

The respite didn't last long, however. By the end of August, Frances was on a plane again for the General Board of Global Ministries Finance Committee meeting. To save time meeting as a committee, Frances led a 90-minute telephone conference call on August 31 of the Development Education subcommittee. This labor-saving technique was still an innovation in 1978.

The first of September found Frances and Don in LeRoy, Michigan, visiting her mom and family and attending her 34-year class reunion at LeRoy High School. As soon as they returned home Don left for a week in California while Fran traveled to UMW linkage events throughout the conference, plus a retreat for Chicago Western District.

Later that month, Fran attended a Women's Division-sponsored Native American Women's Seminar at the Chippewa Reservation in Mount Pleasant, Michigan.

Many requests to speak

As a member of the Women's Division and past conference UMW president, Frances continued to get many requests to speak at local churches and district and conference events. She had much to share about the mission of the church through her general board committee participation. The annual meetings of Global Ministries and the Women's Division typically feature keynote speakers and panel discussions in addition to the ongoing program work.

October was typically "high season" for meetings in The United Methodist Church, and 1978 held true to form for Frances Alguire. Her calendar for the month showed:[10]

Oct. 2	Keynote address to the annual meeting of Central Illinois conference UMW in Bloomington.
Oct. 3	Back to Chicago to present the program for UMW at Grace UMC.
Oct 6-8	Midwest Regional School of Christian Mission committee meeting, Indianapolis.
Oct. 10	Northern Illinois Episcopal Committee, First UMC

in De Kalb.

Oct. 13   North Central Jurisdiction Conference Committee, Dayton, OH..

From Dayton, Frances then went to Pittsburgh, Pennsylvania, for the semi-annual meetings of the Women's Division and Global Ministries, returning home on Oct. 21.

Frances and Donald spent the Oct. 21 weekend together and then he left for a week in Europe. During times away from each other they spoke by telephone daily even though there were no cell phones then. Don was good about keeping in touch and frequently was able to schedule business trips while Frances was away. Fran said Don learned to care for his own needs except for doing laundry. He found it easier to buy new underwear and socks than to press buttons on the washer. The Alguire daughters, whose husbands even ironed shirts, often said, "Mom, you spoil Dad." After nearly 30 years of marriage, however, Frances said "spoiling" her generous and understanding husband was "something I was happy to do."

"Thanksgiving 1978 was a time for special church services and prayers of gratitude to God for our many blessings and a memorable year of serving and sharing," Frances wrote in a remembrance.[11]

Winter works

Since Mary Bond Werner became a widow in 1964, Frances and her sisters had talked her into spending time with them during the winter months. The Alguires were happy to have Mrs. Werner as their guest as the New Year of 1979 began. That January excessive snow fell in the Downers Grove area of Illinois, and drifts stacked up so high on the Alguires' porch roof that it was impossible to see out the upstairs bedroom windows. Don resorted to the treacherous task of shoveling snow off the roof in order to make visibility possible.[12]

The heavy snowfall also caused the cancellation of a few of Frances' regular monthly gatherings. However, in the third week of January she made two trips into Chicago for meetings of the Northern Illinois Conference Episcopal Committee and for the Finance Committee of Garrett-Evangelical Theological Seminary. Don and Fran then made a trip to Coldwater, Michigan, so Mrs. Werner could spend some time with her daughter Kathryn and family.

The frigid weather didn't dampen the Women's Division's agenda, however. In February, Frances spent three days in Denver with other Women's Division leaders training and strategizing in preparation for the 1980 General Conference and Jurisdiction Conference. They had two goals:

* Secure the permanent establishment of the General Commission on the Status and Role of Women, which had been established as an agency in 1976, but still faced stiff opposition in many quarters of the church, and

* Elect a United Methodist woman bishop.

A month later, Frances met with the Northern Illinois Conference Clergywomen's Caucus. By this time, both United Methodist laywomen and clergywomen knew they needed to organize and work together to get women elected to General Conference so they could pass resolutions related to the best interests of women in both church and society.[13]

Frances and Don slipped away for a 10-day winter vacation in Mexico after her Denver trip, but immediately afterward she flew to San Antonio, Texas, where she met with United Methodist Women of the South Central Jurisdiction to plan a regional seminar on world development. At the close of the San Antonio session, Frances was summoned to New York City for a three-day meeting of the General Board of Global Ministries' Finance Committee. She spent the last days of February attending conference committee meetings back in Illinois.

March 1979 came in like a lion for Frances. On the first day of the month, she contributed to a United Nations Association meeting in Chicago, then participated in a United Methodist Women's Stewardship Workshop in Aurora, Illinois. Throughout the month she continued to attend regularly scheduled conference meetings, Garrett-Evangelical Seminary and Center for Parish Development sessions. Frances recalled often being the lone woman at some of these committees, but nonetheless felt free to pose questions and add to the discussions.

More responsibilities

In May 1979, Donald Alguire's business duties expanded significantly when Griffith Laboratories USA announced that his unit, Micro Biotrol Company, has gained so much in U.S. revenue that it was to become a separate company reporting to Griffith International, instead of remaining a division of the American branch. Despite the added responsibility, which meant more separations, Frances said she fully supported Don's promotion, as he supported her church work and other activities. Their hectic schedules made the times they could spend together even more important and necessary to their marriage.

In June, Frances and Don were again lay members of the Northern Illinois Annual Conference, meeting at its traditional site at Northern Illinois University in De Kalb, about two hours west of Chicago. Frances also represented the Women's Division at two Schools of Christian Mission: the Pacific School at Rocky Mountain College in Billings, Montana, and then the Mid West Regional School in Albion, Michigan, which she had helped plan. Her presentations at these meetings highlighted the resources that the Women's Division made available to local and conference units of United Methodist Women, including training in leadership skills, how to initiate and follow through on legislation and how to conduct church-based discussions of human sexuality.[14]

Summer also brought a season for Donald and Frances to renew relationships. They flew to Durham, North Carolina, June 30 until July 3 to spend time with their daughters Mary and Catherine. Back home in Illinois, they hosted a dinner for retiring Bishop and Mrs. Paul Washburn. A few days later Fran served as chef and hostess for a dinner for three of Don's international managers. Later that same week they hosted three more business friends from other countries as house guests, part of their gift for building far-reaching networks of relationships.

Her mother's warning from 18 months earlier that she was doing too much was verified in a physical examination that summer, when Frances' physician told her that "running around to meetings didn't count as exercise." In response to the report, she joined a women's weekly golf group at a nearby country club to exercise her body and a weekly neighborhood ecumenical Bible study group to care for her soul.[15]

International flavors

Barbara Bucholski, a teacher friend from Germany, was the Alguires' guest for four days that August. Frances and Don took Barbara with them to the Werner family reunion in LeRoy, Michigan. They shared a bucolic respite picking wild blackberries, with the Werner family teaching Barbara about life on a large dairy farm.

August was traditionally the time when Don held an annual meeting for Micro Biotrol personnel. Frances always cleared her calendar during this month to support Don and assist with details. Later that month Don and Fran traveled together to Caracas, Venezuela, to meet with business personnel at the Griffith plant. The manager and his wife invited the Alguires to dinner, but their hostess spoke no English and Don and Frances spoke very little Spanish. Despite the language barrier, their hosts were interested in what Frances did, so she explained about her leadership with the Women's Division and the General Board of Global Ministries, along with other volunteer work. They were surprised to learn that at that time, the Women's Division annual contributions amounted to more than $16 million — raised by local UMW units to support missions worldwide. The Venezuelan manager exclaimed: "That's more than our company makes!"[16]

At the end of August, Frances' elderly aunt, Alfrieda Trent, arrived from Albuquerque, New Mexico, for a four-day visit. Fran took Aunt Alfrieda for a visit to the Garrett-Evangelical Theological Seminary in Evanston. When her aunt was introduced to President Neal Fisher, he inquired, "How are you, Mrs. Trent?" Her reply was, "Do you want an organ recital?" Her witty reply was greeted with laughter. Garrett-Evangelical and its faculty and staff impressed Mrs. Trent, who later, with Frances' help, designated a percentage of the Trent estate for an endowed scholarship to the Garrett-Evangelical Seminary. No one knew what that amount might be, but at the time of Mrs. Trent's death her bequest totaled $250,000.

Interest from Alfrieda Trent's endowment has helped Garrett-Evangelical Seminary students ever since. Among the beneficiaries of the Trent scholarship fund was Daniel Wandabula from West Africa, now United Methodist Resident Bishop of the East Africa Area. The future Bishop Wandabula graduated from Garrett-Evangelical in June, 1997, at the same ceremony at which Frances Alguire received an honorary Doctor of Humane Letters degree.[17]

After her aunt departed, Frances and the Northern Illinois conference delegates to the 1980 General Conference met at Euclid UMC in Oak Park. Many in the delegation had asked Frances to serve again as chair, but she consistently declined, knowing what commitments loomed on her horizon.

On Sept. 10, 1979, Frances convened a meeting of the Women's Division Development Education Committee at the Sheraton Hotel in New York City. The committee was preparing to fulfill an ambitious goal outlined two years before: Sending groups of Women's Division directors to visit three areas of the world — Asia, Africa and the Caribbean — to meet with local women involved in health, education, politics, economics and job opportunities. Building on work they had done in world understanding since the 1950s, United Methodist Women wanted to know more about what was happening in the "developing world," and the role that U.S. development played in those countries. The assignment was for each participant in a visiting group to survey a specific aspect of women's conditions in their designated region and report back to the directors. Reports to the Women's Division Board would be followed by Development Education seminars in each of the five U.S. jurisdictions of The United Methodist Church to spread international knowledge throughout the UMW organization.[18]

An Asian sojourn

After the September meeting for Development Education, Frances traveled to Manila, Philippines, with Don for his business. Once again, she seized the opportunity to learn all she could about The United Methodist Church and its work in this southeastern Asian country composed of 7,000 islands.

During the day while Don was conducting business, Frances visited United Methodist missionaries and learned firsthand about their work and ongoing needs. Using her nurse's keen power of observation, she toured the Mary Freebed Hospital and saw its outdated equipment and need for more supplies. She visited schools and talked with students and teachers. She met with the director of a family planning center. From her outings with spouses of Don's Philippines plant managers, Frances learned about Filipino traditions, such as bargaining at the market, local craft works and the skills involved in creating handmade clothing and table linens for which the country is famous.

Her visit to the Philippines also taught Frances an indispensable travel lesson. After venturing out on her own one day for shopping, Frances had forgotten the name of their hotel. She remembered it started with an 'M.' She told the taxi driver she wanted to go to the Mandarin Hotel. As they neared the hotel she knew it wasn't the correct one. She had no way to contact Don, so she asked the cab driver to wait while she entered the Mandarin Hotel to check the telephone yellow pages. She found the right hotel address and was soon back to her room. The incident taught her to carry some hotel identification with her no matter what country she visited — especially those where a language other than English was spoken![19]

The Alguires belatedly celebrated their 30th wedding anniversary in Baguio City north of Manila, then flew on to Bangkok, Thailand, for more of Don's work. The next leg of their Asian journey introduced them to new foods and native cultures, but in the course of travel, Don's checked baggage was lost. He had to manage with the clothes and personal items stowed in his carry-on luggage.

Tony Young, a Chicago employee of Don's, had asked the Alguires to greet his parents in Bangkok. Mr. and Mrs. Young were so pleased to have news of their son that they entertained Fran and Don at an elegant restaurant featuring Thai dancers, and sent an enormous basket of fresh orchids to their hotel room. The next day Mrs. Young came with her driver and a translator to take Frances shopping and for an afternoon of Thai culture. Frances was introduced to chilled fresh coconut milk, sipped directly from the shell, as a refreshing drink on a warm afternoon. That day taught her even more about Thailand, and added to her knowledge of the gracious, thoughtful hospitality practiced in many cultures.

Before traveling on to Indonesia, Frances and Don took a jeep ride north of Bangkok to visit the Hill Tribe people. Everywhere in the village, guides competed to show tourists the local sites, including the private abodes of some families. In one home, the guides pointed out the family's albino child, which repulsed Frances and Don. Frances told the guide that she thought it was not appropriate to make the child into a tourist attraction.[20]

Lost and found

Traveling back to Bangkok, the Alguires' next stop was the airport.

There they searched the lost luggage bin and, to their great relief, found Don's missing luggage. At their next stop, Jakarta, Indonesia, they were met by more international business leaders. By this time, Frances had learned how to take local tours and gain as much information about each country as she could while Don conducted business.

Their Asian sojourn also instilled in Frances the courage of a solo traveler. At first, she said, she didn't like finding restaurants to have lunch on her own, but she reasoned that if she were at home while Don traveled, she'd be eating on her own anyway, since their daughters had long since flown the nest. Her willingness to venture out on her own resulted in a wealth of friendly conversations with English-speaking Indonesians eager to talk with someone from America. Her first Indonesian visit prepared Frances for a future trip back to Jakarta to speak with Indonesian Methodists as the guest of Maimunah Natasha, an active World Methodist Council leader.

When the Alguires returned from their trip to Asia Oct. 3, 1979, Frances became instantly immersed in committee activities. As a Northern Illinois delegate to both General and Jurisdictional Conferences, Frances had been named to chair the program committee for the jurisdictional event. Two days after returning from Asia, she chaired a committee meeting, then met with the local arrangements committee in Dayton, Ohio, where the conference was to be held. The remainder of her October calendar burst with duties at Hinsdale UMC, the annual fall board meetings for Global Ministries and Women's Division, helping plan a retirement event for Bishop Washburn the following June, another meeting in Indianapolis with committee members for the Mid West Regional School of Christian Mission, and a session of the North Central Jurisdiction Council on Ministries.[21]

Few diplomats traveled as widely or carried as thick a portfolio of duties as Frances Alguire did during these years, but one of her greatest challenges lay ahead on the continent of Africa.

On to Africa

Frances joined a group of twelve Women's Division staff and directors in New York City on Nov. 5, 1979, for their last-minute briefing on details — including learning a few Swahili phrases — for their

Development Education Committee's trip to Africa. Prepared with previous inoculations, malaria tablets and other medications, and carrying their passports and tickets, the group departed John F. Kennedy International Airport in the evening Nov. 6 on an Air France flight and landed the next morning in Paris, the fabled "City of Lights."

After a bit of sightseeing the previous evening — in part to help turn their biological clocks forward for the remainder of the trip — the group walked a short distance the next morning from the Hotel Montalenbert to the headquarters of the United Nations Educational, Scientific and Cultural Organization, known as UNESCO. A morning appointment had been previously scheduled with Helga Barraud, a senior staff member,[22] who told them of UNESCO's work in Africa.

Madame Barraud emphasized that time played tremendous factor in development work in Africa, particularly because so many people in Africa are illiterate. UNESCO provided teachers at the request of African countries to work with counterparts at the nations' ministries of education After people became literate, she said, UNESCO provided newspapers with local news and helpful information such as health facts, when to plant seeds, etc. Nonetheless, Mme. Barraud said, "You cannot teach people about environmental education in five years if it normally takes twenty."[23]

The next morning the group returned for another briefing session by UNESCO personnel who had worked in several countries in Africa. Education was the key to African development, the Women's Division group learned, not only in literacy but education for production, understanding government regulations related to import/export, care of machines, health and disease prevention, diet, need for pure water, and means of disseminating information so learning could be shared with each other. Sharing knowledge, even at a rudimentary level, could help an entire village, Frances learned. Thus reading programs were designed to link information to a specific development need such as better health or farming.

Prepared with necessities

That evening, the Women's Division group departed Paris for Dar Es Salaam, Tanzania, arriving in the early afternoon the next day, Saturday,

Nov. 10. While rooming at the Kilimanjaro Hotel for the next four days sounded romantically exotic, Frances said they had been told to pack soap, facial and toilet tissue because such basic hygiene supplies were scarce or unavailable. It proved fortunate that they had come prepared.

That afternoon Frances met with Director Helena Lfliakos at the Young Women's Christian Association, who was in charge of hostel accommodations for young girls and a daytime secondary school. This facility was for young girls coming to the city to learn job skills in fabric dyeing and dress making, food preparation and nursery school operations in cooperation with UNESCO training. Some of their long-range programs were to teach economics, poultry keeping, gardening, bread-making and housekeeping in programs with family connections.

On Sunday, when many shops were closed and driving was not allowed without a special permit, Frances and her companions walked through the city market and saw fresh produce stands loaded with limes, pineapples and tomatoes in abundance. At 11 o'clock they attended a Lutheran Church international service. The ten members of the United Methodist group made up a third of the congregation worshiping in the old decaying structure left by the Germans who colonized Tanzania, previously called Tanganyika. After lunch at the hotel, the group climbed into three cabs for a tour of the city: Dar Es Salaam University; an African village off Bagamoyo Road showing various types of huts found in different parts of the country; a stop to observe Makonde wood carvers; a visit to cashew nut orchards and a look at a brewery using kettles to brew beer from cashews and fruit, reportedly ready to drink in two days' time.

Poor people's hotel

After a visit to the National Museum to learn of Tanzania's history, the group dined at the Rungway Beach Hotel bordering the Indian Ocean. Supposedly the hotel had been developed "so poor people would have a place to go," as one of the group's guides said, but the condition of the hotel clearly showed that economically it did not appear to be making a success. The contrast was especially noticeable when the cab erroneously drove the group to the elegant Bahari Beach Hotel just a few miles away from Rungway Beach. Their guides bragged that Doudi Richardo, an English/Irish gentleman, had been living at the Bahari Beach Hotel since

1951 and had been involved in its development.

Through their visits to the two contrasting hotels, the Women's Division group saw that building roads and bridges had been a greater priority for the country than human development. Still, human conditions had improved in villages that had with a better water supply and adequate primary schools for children grades one through seven. Newspapers were only available in large cities and medical treatment was free through government hospitals where the emphasis was on preventive care.[24]

Key to prosperity: Education

The following morning, Monday, Nov. 12, Frances was one of six participants to visit with Dr. Youssuf Kassam, director of the University of Dar Es Salaam's Adult Education program, and a Mr. Nindi from the Ministry of Education Functional Literacy Section. The two leaders told their Women's Division visitors that they wanted to use adult education to foster lifelong learning in Tanzania, in hopes of eliminating illiteracy, poverty and disease. Mr. Nindi added that when adults know how to produce goods, whether farming, manufacturing or other services, they raise both their own job skills and the economy of their country.

Next the group traveled to the Tanzanian Christian Council offices and met Dr. Janet Craven a member of the Anglican church from Scotland. Frances asked her, "How did a physician from Scotland end up serving in Tanzania?" Dr Craven said when she was eight years old, her parish priest said one Sunday that "he wished someone from the parish would enter the mission field." With the God-given insight sometimes accorded to children, Janet said she knew then that she was that person. She added, "A Youth for Christ program from the USA moved me to Christian commitment."

Dr. Craven gave the Women's Division group statistics of the number of patients treated, her work in prenatal and obstetrics care, health education for village workers and the number of health dispensaries available. She told her visitors that in "olden days" the government recruited medical staff from abroad, but that by the time of their visit the government had begun training indigenous medical workers. The group observed a class session for student nurses.

By this time, the Christian Council's projects were evolving from constructing buildings to meeting village needs, which meant improving the lives of women gathering water and doing gardening and harvesting. Sadly, Tanzania's men had shown no interest in improving women's lives, even though entire villages often depended upon the women's work for their very lives. Health concerns for both women and their communities included safe water and the elimination of cholera and typhoid. A five-year plan was intended to provide clean water for total population and eliminate two of the deadliest dangers to public health: trachoma and diarrhea. However, by 1999, twenty years after Frances Alguire visited Tanzania with the Women's Division, only 45 percent of the rural population and 68 percent of the urban population had access to a clean, safe water supply — statistics that prove UNESCO's estimate regarding how much time is needed to make improvements.[25]

At the time of the Women's Division group's visit, Tanzania was listed as one of the 30 poorest nations in the world, suffering from a lack of natural resources, a sparse population spread over a geographically large area, and a culture that often placed obstacles in the way of accomplishment. In sharing their respective observations, the group learned much that they would apply to the remainder of their African tour, Frances said.

Although suffering with chills, fever and a deep cough by Nov. 13, Frances persevered in her duties, treating her symptoms with aspirin, bottled soda and a few extra hours of rest. She attended the group's meeting with a representative of the tourism ministry, who cautioned the travelers against tipping workers for their service. Frances said she thought this policy was wrong, when baggage handlers and others obviously needed the money. That evening Frances presented a UMW mission pin to Tanzania's YWCA president, one of their local hosts, before packing for an early morning flight to Lusaka, Zambia.[26]

Bombings and history

In Lusaka, the Women's Division group stayed at the Ridgeway Hotel, where they were briefed about assignments to visit as many agencies as possible. Frances was with the group visiting the African American Institute. There, Louise Africa briefed them about bombings in residential areas over the previous month. They also learned that a Botswana-

Zambia ferry and two bridges in the north had been blown up. Louise attributed the bombings to "Rhodesians trying to destroy their enemy." At the time, members of two resistance groups, Zimbabwe African People's Union and Zimbabwe African National Union, were residing in Zambia, using it as a base from which to conduct their efforts to free Rhodesia from British rule. The episode gave the Women's Division visitors a taste of the political turmoil under which Africans often live.[27]

While visiting Zambia, Frances learned that U.S. Agency for International Development funds were used to assist refugees from the Republic of South Africa with post high school technical and vocational training. The refugees had fled from the repressions of South Africa's official system of racial segregation known as apartheid. Among the programs offered were water and sanitation, small industries, development of cottage industries and government central coordinating in education.

Clarence Hall reported on the work of the World Health Organization in Zambia in training nurses and doctors in community health, and training paramedics in both curative and preventive medicine. WHO sanitary engineers assisted the government with water programs in the rural areas where health and nutrition were taught along with literacy and agriculture. WHO also sponsored a six-week primary health care program through which entire communities learned about education, communication, nutrition and immunization.

Returning to their hotel, the Women's Division group exchanged reports on the development agencies they'd visited, along with reports from books about Africa assigned to participants to read in advance. Frances was preparing to give her book review in Kenya.

'Facing Mount Kenya'

Frances and fellow travelers departed Zambia mid-morning Nov. 15 for a four-hour flight to Nairobi, Kenya. Registering at the New Stanley Hotel, the group gathered that evening to hear Frances' lengthy report on the book, "Facing Mount Kenya," written by Jomo Kenyatta in 1938 and republished in 1965. Considered the father of modern Kenya, Kenyatta — whose original tribal name was Kamau wa Ngengi — was the grandson of a Kikuyu medicine man. He converted to Christianity in 1914 and was baptized as John Peter, a name he later changed to

Johnstone Kamau. He adopted the name Jomo Kenyatta, roughly meaning "son of Kenya," in the mid-1930s.[28]

About that time, after working as a civil servant and newspaper editor,
Kenyatta entered the London School of Economics, where he eventually
pursued a degree in anthropology, studying with the world renowned
Polish anthropologist Bronislaw Malinowski. Malinowski was noted for
his achievements in ethnography, or the study of tribal and ethnic
groups, and in reciprocity, or how people exchange goods and labor in
informal economic systems.[29] As a result of his study with Malinowski,
Kenyatta produced "Facing Mount Kenya," which gives an insider's
account of the life and death, work and play, sexual practices and family
relationships of his Kikuyu ethnic group, the largest in Kenya.

Thus Frances Alguire gave the Women's Division travelers a report
from one of the 20th century's greatest leaders of African independence
on how he viewed the culture in which he was formed and lived. In
addition to his explanations of life among the Kikuyu, Kenyatta also
used "Facing Mount Kenya" to reflect on land tenure, economic life and
religion. For instance, among the Kikuyu, cattle represented a display of
wealth. Each family had several sheep and goats, but to own a cow was a
sign of wealth. Economically, wealth was traditionally produced through
farming, hut building, wood carving, basket weaving and dressmaking,
with produce or goods exchanged by barter.[30]

'Pulling together'

By the time the Women's Division group visited Kenya, the country
had been independent of its British colonizers for about 16 years under
Jomo Kenyatta's leadership. The father of his country had died the year
before Frances and her fellow travelers arrived, and had been succeeded
by Daniel arap Moi as president. The national motto of Kenya,
"Harambee" (meaning "pulling together" in Swahili), refers to Kenyatta's
plea for white settlers to remain after independence and "pull together"
with the country's black majority to create a new nation.[31] This was a
much more enlightened policy than some other African leaders who
sought to force out their white citizens, many of whom had lived in
Africa for three generations or more. In the spirit of "Harambee,"
Kenyans continue to volunteer each year in hundreds of communities to

build schools, clinics, and other needed facilities and to collect money to send deserving students abroad for higher education.

During the Kenya visit, Development Education committee members met with the National Council of Women and spent time at the Department of Social Services and heard their concerns for more housing, the need for jobs and sewer systems. The group visited schools, learning that education was free only until grade six. They saw cottage industries and visited a Masai village.

By Nov. 20, the group was ready to return home. Before Frances finished packing her suitcase and souvenirs, however, she received a telephone call from the Women's Division New York office. Deputy General Secretary Theressa Hoover, the Women's Division top executive, called with an unexpected request: "Frances, since you are already in Nairobi, can you stay one more week and meet with the United Methodist Africa Church Growth and Development Committee as a representative of the Women's Division?"[32]

Ms. Hoover's call came on a Tuesday, and the new committee members would be arriving on Sunday. That meant Frances would be alone in Nairobi for four days. Before Frances had embarked on her Africa trip, her mother had worried: "Why are you going to Africa? There is so much trouble there." Frances had assured her mother that she would be safe with a group, but now things looked much different. Her next task was to call her husband with the news.

A new duty in Africa

Frances was surprised to be asked to take on another responsibility, but she was always willing to do what she could for others. She called Don from Nairobi to discuss the details. After conversing together, they decided this was something Frances should do. Don agreed to make business calls by himself in Europe the following week and meet her in Amsterdam on her flight home. This decision meant that Frances said good-bye to the Women's Division Development Education committee members and remained on her own for four days until The Africa Church Growth and Development team members arrived. Her final words to Don were, "Tell my mom I'm fine and send love to her, but don't tell her I'm here alone!"[33]

The first meeting of the Africa Church Growth and Development Committee took place Nov. 24-30, 1979 in Nairobi, Kenya. Committee members (from left) were Gertrude Conteh (Sierra Leone), Frances M. Alguire (USA), Naomi Maryoki (Nigeria), Chadreque Miyongue (Mozambique), Dr. Joyce Mathison, United Methodist missionary in Nigeria, Manuel Torres (Angola) and Mr. Torres' Portuguese interpreter.

Frances' daughters Mary and Catherine provided an insight into why their mother would be willing to stay by herself in an unfamiliar country, awaiting a task that would confront her even more with the staggering needs of the African continent.

"Growing up on a small rural farm, in a close-knit family, and going through the Depression times of having food and shelter but not much else, provided Mom with the awareness of human struggle, the strength that comes from love and the strong belief that things can get better if you work hard enough at it," they wrote in a remembrance. "Seeing her parents help others who were in more need, gave Mom a sense of compassion and self confidence, which she made an effort to convey to inspire others to do likewise. This rural upbringing gave her appreciation that not all knowledge comes from formal education, reminding us that we 'are all equal under God' and often adding "- men AND women" during times when women's issues were a focal topic. Both learning and opportunities were seen as God-given gifts through which one might better oneself for the service of others and the world."[34]

When she agreed to wait for the African Church Growth and

Development Committee, Frances had been in Nairobi long enough to know her way around. After going to the airline office to reschedule her flight, Frances had free time to walk to the nearby market, deal with street vendors, and enjoy fresh air and sunshine. She felt at home, but soon realized from the looks of other pedestrians that she was the only white person in the neighborhood.

That Thursday was Thanksgiving Day in the United States. In the lobby of the New Stanley Hotel Frances saw a U.S. couple. They exchanged greetings as another American couple approached. After conversing a bit and learning why Frances was there, one of the gentlemen asked if Frances would join them for Thanksgiving dinner at the hotel. His wife promptly said, "I've made reservations for four." Frances had her Thanksgiving dinner later that day seated alone at a table that had five place settings. Despite her isolation, Frances gave thanks that her parents had taught her early in life about the gift of hospitality and the joy in breaking bread together. "November 1979 is one Thanksgiving Day that I will long remember," she said.[35]

Helping newcomers

The following Sunday, Frances moved from the New Stanley Hotel to the Milimani Hotel and was present to welcome General Board of Global Ministries staff and Africa Church Growth and Development committee members. The group included 27 Africans, representatives from Germany and Switzerland, and 11 Americans plus Frances, including observers from the General Council on Ministries and the governing committee of The Advance for Christ and His Christ, a program of "second-mile" designated mission giving. The ever-hospitable Frances was able to help the newcomers find a bank for currency exchange, and the Post Office where telephone calls were made. Visitors were also eager to learn which direction to go for souvenirs, and especially relished how easy it was to purchase many beautiful wood carvings.

Regular programs and projects in Africa continued to need ongoing support, but the Africa Church Growth and Development Committee was set up to define programs in evangelism, leadership development, and church growth that needed extra funding. The committee enabled decision-making and funding of projects in less time than is possible in the regular Advance program, where decisions on what will be funded depends entirely on the amount of donors' contributions.

The committee's first meeting in Nairobi was a time of getting acquainted, hearing needs and concerns and discussing procedures. Frances felt fortunate to have as her roommate Irene Chitsiku, a school principal from Zimbabwe, who could help explain the context of many requests to her. The group was invited for dinner and an evening program at the Nairobi Methodist Center by host Bishop Lawi Imathiu of the Methodist Church of Kenya. They also toured the outlying area of the city, viewing unemployment, inadequate housing, and the need for water and sanitary improvements. The committee realized that many years of work lay ahead.

A stolen speech

January 1980 began with Frances attending General Conference delegates' briefing, planning for Bishop Washburn's retirement, and participating in Northern Illinois Conference Council on Ministries and Board of Missions meetings along with local and district United Methodist Women events. She also participated at her local church Administrative Council retreat and a Second Mile giving session. At each of these events, Frances eagerly shared with her audiences the details of her work with the Women's Division and the General Board of Global Ministries.

During Frances' involvement with so many church activities, Don continued his business travels, trying to schedule them while she was away. Daughters Mary and Catherine had graduated with high honors from their respective colleges, and had become employed in their fields respectively in Poughkeepsie, New York, and Boston. The Alguires' family connection remained strong despite their frequent absences from one another. Frances and Don were blessed to have many Hinsdale friends who were hospitable and enjoyed hearing firsthand of their global travels over a meal together.

In early March, Frances was the keynote speaker for the Chicago area World Day of Prayer service held at Euclid Avenue United Methodist Church in Oak Park. The theme, "Responsible Freedom," gave her an opportunity to lift international issues. To emphasize her talk, she wore an African dress she had bought on her recent travels.

Right after the event, she drove from Oak Park to O'Hare International Airport, parked her car in the terminal garage and placed her African dress and speech manuscript in the car trunk. Then she boarded a flight to Indianapolis for a two-day Regional School of Christian Missions committee meeting. Returning to O'Hare on Sunday afternoon, she noticed her car trunk lock had been removed. She notified the police, as she was as concerned about what might have been put into her trunk as what had been removed. The airport authorities had no way of opening the trunk, but did file a report. As Frances was driving home, she remembered there was a button inside the car to open the trunk. Stopping before she entered their garage, she popped the trunk to discover a spare tire missing. Then she noticed that someone had stolen her speech and her African dress! Although dismayed at the loss of her beautiful African costume, she smiled thinking about the stolen speech. She prayed that the robber would read her message and learn about World Day of Prayer.[36]

After the incident of the stolen speech, Frances went on to Dayton, Ohio, in mid-March in her capacity as chair of the North Central Jurisdiction program committee. While in Dayton, she met with members of the Local Arrangement committee to review final details for the July conference. DeWayne Woodring, who at that time also served as business manager of General Conference, was a highly skilled and well-trained convention planner, while the local committee members proved well qualified to carry out many details of the arrangements. Together, their competence helped ease Frances' job considerably.

'Wonderful asset'

After touring the meeting hall in Dayton, Frances was off to the airport for a short flight to Detroit, Michigan, to spend the next week caring for Women's Division and Board of Global Ministries committee work. In addition to their assignments, board members elected to General Conference also met to discuss legislation that needed their support. The group also exchanged information about clergy who were candidates for election as bishop. Frances recalled that being together that week meant having dinners with world church leaders and getting to know them as personal friends. "This was a wonderful asset when debatable issues needed to be voted," she said.[37]

During the Detroit meeting, Frances Alguire's gifts for organization and leading by consensus came to the fore once more as Women's Division and Global Ministries committees met and delegates exchanged information for General Conference.

To help keep the work of the many committees she chaired or served with readily available, the Alguires had invested in yet another five-drawer file cabinet. Frances' precision in keeping track of this information made her an invaluable asset during the Detroit meeting, because she had been able to review, memorize and document data that the committees needed for their work.

In addition, her abilities for helping people discover their gifts, and then ask them to perform tasks using those gifts, enabled her committees to function more efficiently. Frances said she employed a lesson she had learned from an American Management Association member while attending a meeting with Don: No matter how great your idea might be, it would be perfected if reviewed with a group.

Reflecting the light of Christ

During all these meetings, Frances said, she prayed to God for guidance and felt peace and insight from the many people she knew were praying for her. Being a "people person," she said she saw each board member "as a component of a beautiful mosaic reflecting the light of Christ throughout the earth and in ministry to the world." Her goal as a team leader, then, was to reflect the light of Christ she saw in others so that much could be accomplished.[38]

At the conclusion of the 1980 Detroit meeting, Frances shared a cab to the airport with Bishop Emilio De Carvalho of Angola. Their brief sojourn together provided an excellent opportunity for Frances to learn more about Angola in southwest Africa. Back in Downers Grove, Illinois, that evening Fran and Don were reunited at the home of their good friend, Rosalie Herzog, who had previously scheduled a dinner party. They caught up on local news with Tom and Anne Smallwood, Bob and Vivian Miner, and Don's boss and his wife, Carrol L. and Sylvia Griffith.

The next day, a Sunday, Frances drove in the afternoon to a local church in De Kalb District. She had been asked to come and discuss issues scheduled to come before General Conference. When she arrived, however, she discovered that the congregation was more interesting in telling her what they opposed, rather than hearing her speak about what was forthcoming. In particular, the church members gave Frances an earful of their objections to resolutions advocating that The United Methodist Church use "inclusive language" — that is, including both male and female pronouns and images in worship and other settings to refer to both people and God. Her audience that day found the "inclusive language" proposals even more threatening than other legislation seeking to change the denomination's stances against homosexual behavior.[39]

With her characteristic patience, Frances let people vent their fears and misinformation. Her hope was that once their fears were aired, their minds might be open to new ideas. However, inclusive language remained a touchy subject in the church for more than a decade, first in the revision of the United Methodist Hymnal in 1989, and in the adoption of the denomination's first Book of Worship in 1992.

March, 1980 ended with Frances traveling to Evanston for an evening dessert reception for the new president of Garrett-Evangelical Seminary, Dr. Neal F. Fisher. His predecessor, Dr. Merlyn Northfelt, had chosen to retire, and Frances was involved with planning retirement events as well as ceremonies for the new president. In addition, she had been one of the trustees to interview some of the candidates. One of the top three candidates told her later he was amazed at how she had maintained confidentiality in such a complex and sensitive role.[40]

In early April, Frances and Don reveled in a week of family time. Daughter Mary and her husband had relocated to Durham, North Carolina, where he was tops in his law class. Mary was pregnant with their first child. Catherine was also living and working in Durham and had planned a surprise baby shower for her sister. The family reunion was a delightful reprieve from agendas and committee work.

On to General Conference

Returning home from Durham, Frances packed her luggage for 12 days at the 1980 General Conference in Indianapolis April 14-26. Delegates arrived and registered that Monday, and the next day began with an orientation for women delegates, followed by opening worship with Holy Communion at 2 p.m. Legislative committees were then assembled and the work of the conference began.

During General Conference, delegates ran a gantlet of special-interest groups handing out flyers on their respective issues each morning on their way to the convention hall for daily worship. Such handouts aren't permitted inside the convention center. Delegates are seated within "the bar" of the conference, an area of tables and chairs organized according to annual conferences. Volunteer marshals stand guard at the roped-off entrances, allowing only elected delegates, identified by their name badges, to enter. Volunteer pages also congregate at the entrances to pass messages to and from delegates. The proceedings of General Conference are reported in a booklet known as the Daily Christian Advocate. The DCA, as it's known, publishes the results of each day's legislative deliberations, along with all amendments to proposed bills, the agenda for general sessions known as "plenaries," a calendar of events and other announcements.

For those who are elected delegates, Frances recalled, General Conference is like "a big family reunion, meeting many who have served as delegates at other conferences, on general boards and in other arenas."[41] The 1,000 or so delegates, half clergy and half laity, review and either approve or deny thousands of petitions proposing changes in The United Methodist Book of Discipline and the Book of Resolutions.

In addition to its legislative work, the General Conference is also responsible for election of churchwide agencies, including the General Commission on the General Conference, which oversees the organization and operation of each session held once every four years. At the 1980 conference, Frances was elected to a four-year term to the General Commission on General Conference.

Among other actions in 1980, General Conference approved the creation of a General Commission on the Status and Role of Women, one of the Women's Division goals that Frances had promoted. Delegates also approved the special program of the Africa Church Growth and Development Committee to which Frances had been assigned. The committee was charged with raising $7 million for the 1981-84 term to aid

United Methodist churches in Africa. The Advance Committee of the General Board of Global Ministries later took on this fund-raising, setting a $6 million Advance Special goal for churches in the U.S. and Europe, with the United Methodist churches of Africa pledging to raise $1 million.

Jurisdictional Conference

Every four years, United Methodist delegates barely have time to catch their breath after the marathon of General Conference before they face another challenging meeting. During the same week in the summer after General Conference, United Methodists in the United States hold concurrent regional gatherings known as Jurisdictional Conference, mainly for the purpose of electing bishops. In 1980, Frances and Donald were both delegates, so they traveled together to Dayton, Ohio for that year's July 13 to 18 session. As program chairperson, Frances gave her report, introduced her committee members, and expressed her great appreciation to the host committee members. Then she was free to turn her attention to her delegate's duties.

Coming off the successful completion of their agenda at General Conference, United Methodist Women in the North Central Jurisdiction were focused on the second of their two goals: the election of the first woman bishop in the history of Methodism. Frances and other women delegates had thrown their support behind one of the most qualified clergywomen in the jurisdiction, the Rev. Marjorie Swank Matthews.

Like Frances Alguire, the petite Rev. Matthews was born in Michigan, one of six children of a barrel maker. Showing much of the same determination, Rev. Matthews began college at the age of 47, and on graduation from Central Michigan College, chose Colgate Rochester Divinity School because she wanted to study theology in an ecumenical setting. She had been the first woman accepted for probationary ordination in Michigan after the Methodist Church granted full clergy rights to women in 1956, but was not ordained an elder until age 49.[42] With the support of Frances and other delegates, both men and women, Rev. Matthews became the first woman elected a bishop in a major Protestant denomination. She was joined in the class of 1980 by Bishops Emerson S. Colaw and Edwin C. Boulton. Frances was thrilled to be asked to read scripture for the worship service consecrating the newly elected bishops.[43]

When it came time to invest Bishop Matthews with the symbols of her office, conference organizers were embarrassed to find that the official bishop's stole was too long for the petite clergywoman and flowed onto the floor. Bishop Matthews laughed off the episode, saying the too-long stole gave a way to "connect with the people."[44]

After elections were completed, the Jurisdictional Committee on the Episcopacy was charged with the task of assigning bishops to episcopal areas, composed of one or more annual conferences. Frances and two of her colleagues, Revs. Joe Agne and Charles Jordan, had met Bishop Jesse R. DeWitt the previous year while all four of them served on the General Board of Global Ministries. Over breakfast, the three Northern Illinois leaders had quizzed Bishop DeWitt about his leadership style and his positions on Christian social action and ecumenical relations. Their recommendation led to Bishop DeWitt being assigned to the Chicago Area after eight years in Wisconsin, which gladly welcomed Bishop Matthews as its new leader.

'An open mind'

"Fran was a member of the Women's Division of the Board of Global Ministries when I was President of the National Division," Bishop DeWitt, now retired, wrote in a remembrance.[45] "She was one of many who came to the Board during the mid-seventies. Fran faithfully attended all the meetings and participated as a full member of the Board. Unlike some who had specific agendas to accomplish, she entered into the work of the Board with an open mind, a clear vision of who she was and a desire to see the work of the Board and the mission of the Church faithfully administered.

"Representing the North Central Jurisdiction, she was particularly sensitive to racial tensions of the time and the struggle of women for a meaningful participation in the life of the denomination. Her commitment to an inclusive community of faith made it possible for her to take the long view of the Church's mission.

"Over the years our friendship deepened and our experiences in the life of Methodism increased. Fran and Don became close friends as we moved to the Episcopal Office in the Chicago Area. There we shared as family in the work of the Church. We saw their commitment to Christ and the mission of the Church deepen and Fran's influence, as well as her willingness to serve expressed in a variety of ways.

"Fran and Don were involved members of their local congregation and always supportive of their pastoral leadership. Their generosity and commitment called Fran to be a strong advocate for Garrett-Evangelical [Theological] Seminary and its training of individuals for pastoral ministry. She held many meetings in her home where individuals were informed of the seminary's programs and its financial needs."

Back to Africa

The Africa Church Growth and Development Committee met again in Nairobi, Kenya, in January 1981, but development had been on Frances' mind for many months. In August 1980, for one of her many talks, she wrote a "Litany for Development" in which the first letter of each line, when printed, spelled out the word "development."

Litany for Development

Dear Lord God, by whom our roots are nurtured and our life is sustained, we praise your name for your presence that never fails;

Even when we have failed you.

Various people are oppressed, enslaved, dehumanized, and hungry;

Even though you have provided abundantly for all.

Let us share your love and learn to care for all of your creation.

Open our minds and hearts that by your justice we are able to know what justice requires of us.

Prepare our spirits that by your peace we will learn what we must do to be peace-makers.

Make our minds aware of your forgiveness that can bind up this world's wounds and heal our divisions.

Enable our souls to be moved to love you and to follow wherever you lead us.

Nurture us to know that the cry of the poor is for justice, not charity, that we are needed to help build a society in which human rights are safeguarded.

Teach us to be moved to effective personal and corporate action as we respond to you with all we are.

This we pray in the name of Jesus, by the power of the Holy Spirit within us. Amen.[46]

At the Nairobi meeting, Africa Church Growth and Development made its first grants. It awarded $300,000 to some 25 projects — training of all kinds (ministerial, technical and leadership for clergy, women and youth), vehicles for transporting evangelists to rural areas, cassettes and loudspeakers to help spread the word in oral form, an offset press, church and parsonage construction and contributions towards two twin-engine airplanes and a proposed Bible training institute. Other programs approved by the committee as funds became available included scholarships, library books, technical training for youth, agriculture programs to help combat hunger, a youth retreat center and church construction.

Connecting over lunch

By mid-week of this second gathering, Frances Alguire noted that the women were sitting silently with the laymen and clergy members from their annual conferences and didn't mingle with other women, as is typical at most U. S. church meetings. Some of the Africans came from French-speaking areas, while others spoke Portuguese. To help them overcome their shyness, Frances suggested that the women have lunch together the following day. She reserved a table to accommodate them and a lively discussion began with a church member from Switzerland helping with translations.

Over lunch and conversation, Frances and other English-speaking committee members learned that their African sisters wanted to learn how to write funding proposals and be more involved in decision making. The African church women were interested in doing more than cottage industry work and making crafts. They asked for leadership training, and help with ways to participate in the committee's proceedings. In their enthusiastic response to Frances' encouragement, they asked to meet again for the evening meal. In this smaller group, the African women felt free to discuss their ideas for church growth and development, instead of facing conversations in the larger committee where males often dominated. "The next day they gathered again at mealtime and I told them they were doing well without me," Frances recalled.[47] From Frances Alguire's simple act of hospitality, an All-African Women's

Assembly eventually took shape with the help of Rose Catchings, a staff member of the General Board of Global Ministries' World Division assigned to the Africa area.

In addition to helping plan and participate in United Methodist Women's Development Education seminars in each of the five Jurisdictional areas, Frances was in great demand at local churches as a Sunday morning speaker. At each event she shared the many mission needs of Africa and promoted financial support for Africa Church Growth and Development. Appeals throughout the Northern Illinois Conference helped the conference reach its financial pledge of $200,000 toward the original goal of $6 million. The Rev. Dwight Busacca, Global Ministries' field representative for mission development, helped provide information that generated support for African development. As a result, in 1981 the North Central Jurisdiction contributed $121,786, amounting to 55 percent of the total funds raised to that date.

'I'm sorry I don't have more to send'

Frances' persuasive appeals for Africa Church Growth and Development even moved members of her own family. After hearing her grandmother speak at a church one Sunday morning, five-year-old Anna dashed to her room and came back with a handful of coins. "I've saved two weeks' allowance and I want you to take it for food for the hungry people in Africa," she told her astonished grandmother. Anna's contribution totaled one dollar. "I'm sorry I don't have more to send," she added. Deeply moved, Frances told her, "Anna, if every person in the world gave two weeks of their income, the hungry would be well cared for."

Then Anna asked if they had grocery stores in Africa, and soon Frances described to her granddaughter how African women did all the gardening for their families, and often walked long distances for water, medical help and basic supplies. Frances recalled telling Anna that her dollar would be added to those of others to help women in a Kenyan village who cooked on a handmade metal charcoal stove, for supplies at a girls' school in Zimbabwe, and as a donation to women selling baskets in Zaire as a means of earning money for food.[48]

Frances continued to work for Africa Church Growth and Development for several years, but she was dismayed that the worthy projects needing funding always exceeded the available resources. In the laity address to the 1983 session of the Northern Illinois Conference, she said:

"Where is God leading us? Are we hearing the needs of our sisters and brothers in Africa? Are we giving assistance in a manner which aids or retards the development of churches and leaders? As lay people we ask each one present to respond to what has begun in Africa. We ask you to share with others about Africa Church Growth and Development so they may also respond in love and faith."[49]

Women's health

The year 1983 also was significant for Frances in a major event that brought together her training and experience as a registered nurse and her service through the church. Sponsored by the General Board of Global Ministries, an international symposium on women's health met for four days, Nov. 9-12, at the Church Center for the United Nations in New York City. Frances served as chair of the event's planning committee, which included representatives the General Board of Church and Society, the General Commission on the Status and Role of Women and program units of the General Board of Global Ministries: Health and Welfare Ministries, Mission Education and Cultivation, the National Division, the World Division and the Women's Division, the administrative arm of United Methodist Women. Serving with her as chairpersons of other elements of the symposium were Global Ministries staff members Mia Adjali of the Women's Division and Cathie Lyons of Health and Welfare Ministries, along with Bishop H. Ellis Finger Jr. representing the Council of Bishops, and Leigh M Roberts.

Under a bright blue-and-white banner proclaiming "A Woman's Health Is More Than a Medical Issue," the 100 participants came to grips with some of the sobering statistics of women's health around the world in the 1980s. Among the statistics from the World Health Organization posted on the walls of the conference meeting room:

* Two-thirds of all women of reproductive age in developing countries are anemic;

* Two of every three illiterate people are women;

* Women do two-thirds of the world's work, and receive only a tenth

of the world's income.

In addition to these statistics, the conference didn't shirk from confronting other serious threats to women's health:

* Female circumcision and genital mutilation in north Africa;
* Bride burnings in India;
* Rape as a weapon of war; and
* The "Valiumization" of older women in the United States.

"Health has everything to do with women's status in today's world," keynote speaker Dr. Lucille Mair told the conference, according to a New York Times report by Judy Klemensrud.[50] "If a woman's health is not good, she more than likely holds a subordinate status in her society."

Dr. Mair told the gathering that she deplored the "beast of burden" status of women that she had seen in so many countries in Asia, Africa and Latin America.

"You see these women on country roads, mile after mile, bent almost horizontal to the ground as they carry water, firewood or market produce," she said. "Meanwhile, their male companions stride along beside them, upright as the walking sticks they hold in their hands.

"It is a sight that I can never forget," Dr. Mair was quoted by the Times.[51]

A goal not yet met

Cathie Lyons told the New York Times that the purpose of the symposium was to focus attention on the World Health Organization's goal of health for all by the year 2000. Unfortunately, that goal was not met. According to the World Health Organization's web site in 2007:

* One in every 74 women worldwide will die giving birth, while 1 in every 20 women in Africa will die giving birth and 1 in every 46 women in South Central Asia will die giving birth.

* As of the year 2005, the last year for which records had been compiled, women in Afghanistan had a life expectancy of 41 years; women in Zimbabwe could expect to live 42 years; women in the Democratic Republic of Congo had a life expectancy of 48 years; and women in Iraq could expect to live 61 years.[52]

Clearly, the Women's Health Symposium served a major purpose in raising the awareness of the multidimensional factors of women's health, needs that continue to this day.

For Frances Alguire, her service to the women's health symposium led to more representation in the global context. At the 1985 conference that concluded the United Nations' Decade of Women, she returned to Nairobi, Kenya, as chair of the Committee on Women & Health Strategies, representing The United Methodist Church as a non-governmental agency.

According to an article in the July-August 1985 issue of UN Chronicle, some 157 governments were represented at the Nairobi Conference, along with intergovernmental organizations, United Nations bodies and agencies, non-governmental organizations and national liberation movements. More than 80 percent of the 2,000 delegates were women, and women headed approximately 85 percent of the delegations. Among the findings related to Frances Alguire's committee on women's health, the United Nations cited WHO statistics of the time:

> "The World Health organization (WHO) estimates that, excluding China, 25 per cent of people in cities and 71 per cent of those in the countryside of developing countries are without safe drinking water. The consequences are ill health and great hardship for women who often have to walk long distances to fetch water.

> "To keep a family of five in good health, a woman must make about 15 journeys a day to the water source. But many women live a long distance from safe drinking water and can only make one trip a day. In Burkina Faso, for example, some women leave at dusk to walk to the water hole, sleep there overnight and return at dawn. It is not surprising then that 8 million children die each year of diseases that might have been prevented by clean water from a nearby tap."[53]

Once again, Frances Alguire had been among women leaders who pioneered new understandings about the status and role of half the human population.

Manual labor on ballots

For all the seemingly glamorous travel of being a director of the Women's Division and the General Board of Global Ministries, sometimes Frances' responsibilities came down to plain, hard physical work.

Andris Y. Salter, a Women's Division staff member, recalled that she met Frances in 1982 when she first started with the Women's Division as a regional staff. During that time directors living in an area were assigned to work with regional staff. "Since I was new staff it was especially important and helpful to have seasoned staff working to introduce me to the region and the issues within the region, especially since the regional lines [for Women's Division] did not follow jurisdictional lines," Ms. Salter wrote in a remembrance.[54]

Frances, representing Northern Illinois Conference and Mary Carter, from Central Illinois Conference, were assigned to work with Andris in the Evanston region. They helped her develop relationships with United Methodist Women in the Evanston region, and introduced her to the region's special issues.

Their first big project was working with the election process for directors from the North Central Jurisdiction. Fran and Andris organized the election process by collecting information for the profile booklet and mailing list, identifying voting delegates and organizing tellers and ballots.

"It's funny to think about it now, but we spent hours collecting, organizing, typing, collating, stapling and three-hole-punching those booklets, then mailing them to all the delegates," Ms. Salter said. "We spent most of the 1984 meeting, that year in Wisconsin, in a dark coat room manually counting the ballots. We counted those ballots over and over to make sure we would be reporting the correct number. Today all of this is computerized, but I like to think that we 'knew it when.' Thank God those days are over!"[55]

Andris and Frances also spent time together at Garrett-Evangelical Theological Seminary where Frances was a trustee from 1973 to 1983. Frances made sure that Andris participated on the campus in many capacities that shared the work of United Methodist Women. "I remember Fran and Don fondly as very special people," Ms. Salter said. "I appreciate Fran as a special friend who gently introduced this Southerner to the Midwest."

Innovations

Andris Salter's remembrances of the toil of hand-counting ballots in

1984 were just one of the inefficient practices used by The United Methodist Church that sparked Frances Alguire's imagination between 1984 and 1988. A major impetus for one of her major innovations was her experience of the 1984 General Conference in Baltimore, Maryland.

On one hand, the Baltimore conference marked a major celebration for The United Methodist Church – the 200th anniversary of the official founding of the Methodist Church in the United States of America. The logo chosen for the church's bicentennial depicted a large graphic of a circuit rider, or traveling preacher, whose efforts to plant churches along America's frontier led to the Methodist church's rapid growth. The church and the nation went west together.

However, the Baltimore conference also was marked by some of the most divisive tension to date in the church over the issue of United Methodist stances regarding people of homosexual orientation and homosexual behavior. The politicizing of the church's legislative process, along with the polarizing of its doctrine, showed most clearly in the pressure put on General Conference delegates to maintain The Book of Discipline's stance declaring homosexual behavior to be "incompatible with Christian teaching."

Old-fashioned balloting

In 1984, General Conference was still balloting in an old-fashioned manner – by having delegates stand to be counted. While this practice provided clarity regarding a delegate's position on matters before the church, it also left the delegates vulnerable to pressure and even reprisals over their votes. Many delegates felt enormous pressure from special interest groups in the church whose proponents promised to remember how delegates voted and mete out retribution when the delegates returned home.

Because of her experience in helping to plan significant meetings such as the North Central Jurisdiction conference and the women's health symposium, Frances Alguire was named to the 1984-88 General Commission on the General Conference. Unlike program agencies such as the General Board of Global Ministries or the General Board of Discipleship, which deal with many kinds of mission and ministry, the Commission on the General Conference has one task: to plan, organize and administer the next top legislative assembly for the global church.

Frances was chosen to chair the commission, and one of her first recommendations was for DeWayne Woodring, the General Conference business manager, to research the installation of electronic balloting for the 1988 General Conference in St. Louis, Missouri. Frances had seen the effectiveness of electronic balloting through her international work, and its efficiency and privacy contrasted sharply with the cumbersome, vulnerable method used by the church. Mr. Woodring at first resisted the idea, being unsure whether it could be set up in a temporary venue such as the kind of conference centers in which General Conference typically meets.[56]

Frances, however, was determined that there would be no repeat in St. Louis of the kind of political pressure that delegates to the Baltimore conference experienced. At her gentle but firm insistence, and with the commission's backing, Mr. Woodring went to work finding computer experts who could install and administer an electronic balloting system for the St. Louis conference.

By the time delegates arrived in St. Louis in May 1988, the St. Louis Convention Center had been set up with rows of tables at which delegates would be seated, and at each place was a numbered keypad. The system worked well enough during the delegates' initial instruction, but then some sharp mathematicians among the delegates noticed that the vote totals didn't add up properly. Then, as computer systems are wont to do, the system broke down entirely, and for a day or so, any needed votes had by taken by paper ballot.

Shortly thereafter, DeWayne Woodring stood onstage to announce that electronic balloting would resume. He made his announcement by holding up a sheaf of green-and-white lined computer paper, which he opened to a large cutout of an insect. "We found the bug in the system, and we fixed it," he announced to gales of laughter from delegates and spectators alike.[57]

General Conference has taken votes by electronic ballot ever since, and the system has performed well.

Remembering Aldersgate

At the same time Frances Alguire was leading the General Commission on the General Conference, she was serving as president of the North American Section of the World Methodist Council. During this time Methodists worldwide were preparing to mark 1988 as another significant date in Methodist history – the 250th anniversary of May 24, 1738, when John Wesley experienced his "warmed heart" conversion during a Methodist Society meeting at Aldersgate Street.

John's Aldersgate experience came just a few days after his brother and co-worker, Charles, had had a similar heartwarming experience of salvation. The spiritual fire lit in the Wesley brothers at this time became the energy that ignited the Methodist movement.

British Methodists were gearing up for a major observance of the anniversary. Seasoned world traveler that she was by this time, Frances also understood that the celebration the Wesleys' life-changing event could provide a spiritual pilgrimage for American Methodist and Wesleyan adherents to the sites of Methodist history in Great Britain. In response to an invitation from their British cousins, the North American Section agreed to host a special tour in honor of the occasion. The World Methodist Evangelism office, located in the United States, was designated to develop and coordinate the program so that participants not only saw the sights, but felt something of the same spiritual enlightenment and exaltation that John and Charles Wesley had felt.[58]

Tight schedule

The schedule was tight, for to observe the actual date of the Wesleys' conversion, the tour had to leave within a few days after the end of General Conference – May 18-26, 1988. There was one big advantage to the schedule: The tour could be arranged so that the participants would spend Pentecost Sunday 1988 in the New Room, which John Wesley established in 1739 in Bristol, England, as the home of a Methodist Society, in effect the first Methodist church building.

The arrangement for the tour was brilliant. After meeting first in London to see the sights – including Aldersgate Street – the group prepared to board two specially hired trains. In an impressive ceremony at St. Pancras station that included a 200-voice choir, 100 Methodist railwaymen, 500 American Methodists and 500 British Methodist youths, the two trains were named "John Wesley" and "Charles Wesley." The trains took off in alternate directions, one to the north and the other to the west, to visit the "Golden Triangle" of Methodism, including the Epworth Old Rectory, home of the Wesley family, the Epworth Village Church where John's and Charles' father, Samuel, preached, and Samuel's tomb where John stood to preach in the open air.[59]

After three days of touring, the trains converged in Gloucester, England, and the American delegation went on to Bristol for Pentecost. On May 22, two Pentecost worship services took place in the New Room, where the American delegation had the opportunity to join British Methodists and World Methodist leaders for morning and evening worship. The Rev. H. Eddie Fox, World Evangelism director, presided at the morning service at which the Rev. Maxie D. Dunnam, World Evangelism Chair, gave the sermon. Frances presided at the evening service at which Bishop Lawi Imathiu of Kenya preached.

The next day, the tour group returned to London to prepare for a "great day of celebration" for the 250th anniversary of John Wesley's conversion experience. In late afternoon the delegation went to St. Paul's Cathedral for the invitation-only 5 p.m. worship service at which Her Majesty, Queen Elizabeth II, appeared in person to read a proclamation commemorating the historic event. The evening closed with a great open-air celebration that drew thousands to Aldersgate Street to remember God's gift of salvation and faith to his servant, John Wesley.

Those who made the 1988 Aldersgate pilgrimage reported their own hearts were "strangely warmed" by connecting to the beginnings of Methodism.

An unexpected ending

Life for Frances and Donald Alguire continued to be full and busy, as one might expect of a successful, mature couple who had given their lives to their family, their church and their professions. In mid-1987, however, they were thrown one of those "life curves" that sent them in a new direction.

Frances and Don were preparing to host their annual appreciation party for Micro Biotrol Co. employees. While Frances was home in Downers Grove, Illinois, putting the finishing touches on the evening's plans, Don was called into the office of the new president of Griffith Laboratories. His friend, the founder of Griffith Laboratories, had died six months earlier. There he was informed that he was being given an early retirement "package" by the new management of Griffith Laboratories.[60]

Don was utterly shocked, as was Frances, by the news. Don had been one of Griffith Laboratories' most industrious and innovative employees for nearly three decades. His vision and foresight had helped the company evolve from a local business into a multinational corporation for which Don himself managed 17 plants worldwide. Like many seasoned business leaders, however, he suddenly found himself involuntarily retired by management with new plans.

Don had no choice but to take the offer, but an urgent matter loomed: What about the employees' party?

After they consulted with one another, Frances and Don decided they had no choice but to go ahead with their plans. Furthermore, they decided they would say nothing to anyone about Don's impending departure. One can only imagine how they made it through that evening, realizing that the event was actually a farewell to the successful profession that Don had known, and Frances had supported, throughout the majority of their marriage.

Frances, with Don behind the camera, hosts a group of Stephen Ministers at their home in Chapel Hill, North Carolina, a scene typical of their hospitality.

No reason to stay

Once their heads had cleared a bit, they realized that there was no reason for them to stay in Downers Grove any longer. Their daughters
Mary and Catherine were adult women with families of their own, and
Frances and Don were no longer tied to Don's work. So they marshaled
their resources and returned to Michigan, where they built their dream
home in New Buffalo on the eastern shore of Lake Michigan. Still too
young to sit in rockers beside the fireplace (which was never their style
anyway), Don and Frances started their own business, Ageless Artifacts,
buying and selling antiques and collectibles at local antique malls. They
joined First UMC in New Buffalo and soon were active with church
meetings. Fran soon was made president of the UMW and Don later
became chair of the Church Administrative Council. Fran became an
active member of the West Michigan Annual Conference and chaired
her local church Committee on Missions.[1]

Finishing her term as president of the North American Section of the
World Methodist Council, Frances was elected to the Presidium, the
Council's officers, at the 16th World Methodist Conference in Singapore
in 1991. Back home, she was chosen president of United Methodist
Women at First UMC in New Buffalo for the 1992-96 term. She also
became active in the New Buffalo Service League, where she served as
chaplain for four years.

Thus, after the shock of Don's enforced retirement, Frances and
Donald Alguire resettled themselves into an active, fulfilling new life. Yet
at a time when most retirees were enjoying less responsibility and more
leisure, Frances' and Don's greatest service to Christ's Church still lay
ahead of them.

Frances and Bishop Forrest Stith go over plans for the Mission Linkage event in 1981.

Frances wore her Africa dress to Hinsdale UMC to give a report on the work of the Africa Church Growth and Development Committee. Not long after this photo was taken, her outfit and her speech were stolen from her car trunk.

In 1987, while president of the North American Section of the World Methodist Council, Frances Alguire participated in the ceremony marking the union of two churches to form the Evangelical Lutheran Church in America, along with Chicago Area United Methodist Bishop Jesse DeWitt. In a rare appearance in ecclesiastical garb, Frances wore the doctoral robe of Methodist theologian Georgia Harkness, who had bequeathed it to Garrett-Evangelical Theological Seminary. Frances had been associated with the seminary as a trustee and development officer for nearly 15 years when this photograph was taken.

SYMPOSIUM ON

women & Health

"A Woman's Health Is More Than a Medical Issue"

The 1983 Symposium on Women and Health was a groundbreaking event for the General Board of Global Ministries. Frances Alguire served on the planning team for the symposium and helped shape the program.

Women's Health Discussed As a Worldwide Problem

Sithembiso Nyoni

Sheila Sundaram

Dr. Erlinda Senturias

Dr. Lucille Mair

Dr. Leila Mehra

By JUDY KLEMESRUD

Women from the United States and third-world countries gathered in New York this past week to plead for improvements in women's health around the globe.

They spoke of circumcision of girls in northern Africa, of bride-burnings in India, of rapes of women by soldiers in Africa and of what they called the "Valiumization" of older women in the United States.

"Health has everything to do with women's status in today's world," said Lucille Mair, a native of Jamaica who is secretary general of the United Nations conference on the Palestinian question. "If a woman's health is not good, the more than likely holds a subordinate status in her society."

Dr. Mair was the keynote speaker at a four-day conference called Women and Health, sponsored by the General Board of Global Ministries of the United Methodist Church and held at the Church Center for the United Nations, 777 United Nations Plaza.

'Woman as Beast of Burden'

Dr. Mair told the audience she deplored the "syndrome of woman as beast of burden" that she had seen in some countries in Asia, Africa and Latin America.

"You see these women on country roads, mile after mile, bent almost horizontal to the ground as they carry water, firewood or market produce," she said. "Meanwhile, their male companions stride along beside them, upright as the walking sticks they hold in their hands."

"It is a sight," she added, "that I can never forget."

Cathie Lyons, the United Methodist Church official who planned the conference, said one of its major purposes was to identify the most important women's health issues, so that when the United Nations Decade for Women ends in 1985, the church can continue to work in the area of women's health.

movement will take place unless women's health is focused on," Miss Lyons said, "because women are half the population, and they are the poorest segment of the population."

The 100 participants from women's and church groups throughout the country met in a conference room dominated by a blue-and-white banner the length of a subway car that said, "A Woman's Health Is More Than a Medical Issue." Nearby, a poster listed the following statistics from the I.L.O.: Two-thirds of all women of reproductive age in developing countries are anemic; two of every three illiterate people are women; women do two-thirds of the world's work and receive only a tenth of the world's income.

Underneath the banner, speaker after speaker told of the poor health conditions of the world's 2.2 billion women, 75 percent of whom live in developing countries.

A Problem Ingrained in a Culture

Although female circumcision was first brought to worldwide attention in 1980 during the World Conference of the United Nations Decade for Women in Copenhagen, the practice continues to be a problem in several countries in northern Africa, according to Dr. Leila Mehra, a native of India who is with the World Health Organization in Geneva.

The women allow it to be done to their daughters because it is so deeply ingrained in the culture," she said. "But it can cause very serious physical and emotional problems for these girls in their later health lives."

Sheila Sundaram, a consultant to the Natl

born, because families generally don't want female children.

"The female infant in India is neglected, poorly fed and has very little opportunity for nurture or preschooling," she said. The poor nutrition continues when the woman marries and eats only the leftovers after her husband and children have been fed, she added.

Mrs. Sundaram said that fatal burnings of brides as a result of their dowry problems have reached an "epidemic proportion" in India. She said that these have averaged one

In many third-world countries they are virtual beasts of burden.

case of bride burning almost every 12 hours.

"When a girl gets married a certain amount of money is expected," she explained. "Certain families want more and more, and when a bride cannot get it, she often pours the kerosene used in cooking on herself and commits suicide, because in India she cannot go home. Or else the in-laws

Sithembiso Nyoni, a rural development consultant in Bulawayo, Zimbabwe, said that in her country and other African countries such as Chad, Uganda, Mozambique, Angola and Namibia (the disputed territory also known as South West Africa), where there are many military people among the civilian population, more and more women were being beaten and raped by armed servicemen.

"More often than not nothing is done to these men," she said. "They are mere pro-

tested by law than the civilian women. Sometimes if women report any beatings or rape cases they are in further danger from these armed men for having reported them to the authorities."

Mrs. Nyoni asserted that women and children in Zimbabwe had been the victims of experimentation with drugs for birth control,

ing of its dangers," she said. "The result was that several women who used it for many years suffered serious side effects, when one woman dared to complain, she was told, 'No woman has dropped dead yet as a result of using it.'"

Tish Sommers of Oakland, Calif., president of the 7,000-member Older Women's League, charged that some doctors too readily prescribe Valium and other mood-altering drugs for older women who are not physically ill.

"A major shift away from doctors and drugs would be beneficial for older women," she said. She urged that these women take more responsibility for their own health through diet, exercise and avoidance of drugs and alcohol.

Dr. Urbinda Senturias, a health official with the National Council of Churches in the Philippines, told of the success in that country of the Community Based Health Program, in which health workers live with the inhabitants of rural communities. The program is in about 100 communities, she said.

Opposition From the Military

Dr. Senturias said that members of the military, loyal to President Ferdinand E. Marcos, generally oppose the program "because we do things like question why 35 percent of our health budget goes for a nuclear reactor and other energy projects."

Several speakers at the conference said they thought women's health would be improved when women became policy makers in male-dominated health-care systems and in more women-centered medical schools.

Dr. Louise Branscomb, an obstetrician-gynecologist in Birmingham, Ala., and a member of the board of admissions of the University of Alabama Medical College, offered a ray of sunshine. "Please do not pat too much hope on the women medical students," she said. "When a woman first comes into the

Health and Welfare Ministries Program Department / Bishop H. Ellis Finger, President / John A. Murdock, Associate General Secretary

'Health for All'

Program Department challenges church to make health concerns a priority and to provide direct health services where needed.

A Woman's Health Is More Than a Medical Issue

In 1975 the United Nations proclaimed the Decade of the Woman, and in 1980 women from throughout the world gathered in Copenhagen to prepare for the final international conference in Nairobi in 1985.

This focus on the special problems of women in today's society was refined and amplified as a special concern of the Health and Welfare Ministries Program Department during the past year.

Health and Welfare expanded upon this transnational theme in October by adopting as a quadrennial concern the World Health Organization's campaign for "Health for All by the Year 2000."

What does this mean? Perhaps it is easiest to define what it does not mean. A preliminary document sent to participants of the Symposium said that the goal of health for all "does not mean that in the year 2000 doctors and nurses will provide medical repairs for

everybody in the world for all their existing ailments; nor does it mean that in the year 2000 nobody will be sick or disabled."

Rather both of these themes mean that health care will begin closer to home. For it is at home and in places of employment where the individual has control over his or her health. It means education and advocacy programs to reach people that ill health is not inevitable. It creates a growing awareness of preventive health care tech-

The Christian CENTURY

CELEBRATING OUR CENTENNIAL 1884 ✦ 1984

JANUARY 25, 1984

SPECIAL REPORTS

Women and Health: More Than a Medical Issue

Press reports testify to the significance of the Women's Health Symposium.

THE UNITED METHODIST REVIEW

Frances Alguire

Frances Alguire is delegate to assess progress of women

Frances M. Alguire, of Downers Grove, is one of 21 United Methodists going to Nairobi, Kenya, in mid-July to assess progress made by women worldwide during the last ten years.

They are representatives to Forum 85, a gathering arranged by 60 non-governmental organizations to parallel the official United Nations Conference to Appraise the U.N. Decade for Women. The forum will evaluate progress made on the goals of equality, development and peace, and formulate strategies looking toward the year 2000.

Mrs. Alguire was designated by the Board of Global Ministries as a representative in the Health and Welfare Department. She chairs the Committee on Women in Health, who will be presenting a panel on global issues entitled "Women's Health is More than a Medical Issue."

She and her husband, Donald, were in Vienna, Austria last fall for a pre-decade planning committee session. The Alguires are members of Hinsdale UMC.

NIC represented at World Methodist meet

Frances M. Alguire, member of Hinsdale UMC is seen with Faatauvaa Tapuai, President of the Methodist Church in Samoa. Ms. Alguire introduced the President to members of the Social and International Affairs Committee (SIAC) at the recent meeting of the executive committee of the World Methodist Council in Brussels, Belgium.

Mrs. Alguire moderated a panel on "South/North Dialogue and Solidarity with the Poor." A consultation on the South/North poverty issue is planned in October of 1983 in Barbados.

Another major issue of concern of this committee is peace and disarmament. Dr. Kenneth Greet, Secretary of the British Methodist Conference, and a member of SIAC, presented a paper on this topic with reference to his new book THE BIG SIN, dealing with Christian faith and disarmament.

SIAC will meet again in September of 1984 and formulate a draft of an international social creed.

Frances Alguire's increasing involvement in international issues on behalf of The United Methodist Church was documented by several newspapers.

Aldersgate 250th Anniversary Tour

Wesley Memorial Methodist Church, Epworth

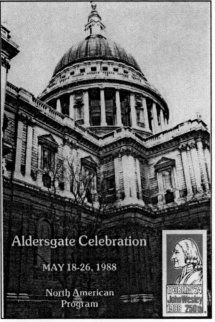

Aldersgate Celebration

MAY 18-26, 1988

North American Program

One of the major accomplishments of Frances Alguire's term as president of the North American Section of the World Methodist Council was this tour in celebration of the 250th anniversary of John Wesley's conversion at Aldersgate. American Methodists accepted the invitation of British Methodists to join in marking the occasion with several significant worship services, including a service at St. Paul's Cathedral attended by Her Majesty, Queen Elizabeth II. The tour also observed Pentecost with morning and evening worship at the New Room in Bristol, purchased and used by John Wesley as the first Methodist church.

Chapter 4

'God Trusted a Woman'

Set inside a walled garden, the international headquarters of the Catholic lay association, The Community of Sant'Egidio, offers an island of spiritual calm amid the bustle of Rome's Trastevere neighborhood. Dr. Frances M. Alguire, the newly elected Chair of the World Methodist Council, approached the microphone at Sant'Egidio's 1996 International Conference on Peace and Religion, and began her talk on the conference theme, "Which Humanism for 2000?"

"Greetings!" she said. "Greetings to you, male and female! Greetings to you, youth, adult, oldster! . . . Greetings to you, regardless of your character, your color, your creed, your race, your religion, your nationality, your health or your abilities."[1]

Moments later Dr. Alguire, in her first public representation as Chair of World Methodism, spoke these words:

"God trusted a woman to carry the Son of God for nine months. I believe we should not deny women the opportunity to share the word of God. For too long, secular and societal groups have denied the full participation of women. In many areas, women are still considered inferior products of God's creation. We must work for opportunities for women to participate more fully and freely without men feeling threatened by their participation."

The audience burst into applause, and in moments, the entire crowd, including Dr. Alguire's co-panelists, were on their feet in acclamation.

With that declaration of faith and future, Frances Alguire set the course for her 1996-2001 term as the first laywoman to be chairperson of the 32-million-member World Methodist Council.

First woman in 115 years

Frances Alguire's assertion that women deserved to be in church leadership could hardly have been more important or more poignant, considering that she was the first woman elected to lead the World Methodist Council in its 115-year history.

First known as the Methodist Ecumenical Council, the organization was founded in 1881 with a gathering in London, England. No less an

American authority than *The New York Times* professed itself skeptical of the new body's aims and effectiveness:

"It has been [John] Wesley's push which has filled America with his disciples and carried Methodism to the ends of the earth. It has overrun the world like Mohammedanism. It has done and is doing a service of the greatest importance to humanity. But this should not render its leaders blind to the fact that the system is without any proper theological or historical basis, and only its cohesive Church polity and its enthusiasm for the CHRIST hold its conglomerate masses together. Here lies its danger. It is always controlled in its directions by the religious body which is the strongest. . . . Out of this characteristic arises a difficulty, for it has not the same power to keep people as to win them. This difficulty is partly social because the middle is always rising in the case of individuals into the higher class, but it is also theological or moral, and it arises from the fact that Methodism is a Church by the accident of position, or as an after-thought. This is a disintegrating force that stands out more and more clearly as Methodism aspires to be the church of the future. . . . It will be one of the problems of the approaching Council to solve the question whether Methodism, pure and simple, can exist upon the basis of a broad and liberal education. . . ."[2]

Obviously, the New York Times had never read Charles Wesley's dictum that one of the purposes of Methodism was to "unite the pair so long disjoined - knowledge and vital piety!"

'The World's Methodist Council'

A September 15, 1881 *New York Times* headline may be the earliest print reference to the body as "The World's Methodist Council."[3] The article begins with a quote from the *London Times* praising the event: "The Methodist Ecumenical Conference offers, in some very important points, favorable comparison with other religious conferences. There is really no sign of squabbling. The common resolution to do as much good as possible is so universal and strong that it overpowers petty selfishnesses which create so much friction in other more elaborate machines."

The article concluded with a report on the issue of higher education that had exorcised the *New York Times* when the conference started: ". . . to-day the discussion was on the higher education demanded by the necessities of the Church in our times, the duty of the Church to maintain schools which are Christian in their character and influence, etc. All the speakers expressed a strong feeling in favor of education of the young. Bishop Holsey (colored) said he rejoiced at the movement as tending to improve the condition of his race."[4]

These first reports on the Methodist Ecumenical Council showed that from its beginnings, the body had a high concern for education, which continues to this day through Methodist-related schools, colleges and universities worldwide. The reports also show, albeit sketchily, that the Council was a racially inclusive body from its beginnings, a theme that has continued throughout the Council's existence.

However, there remained a glaring omission: Despite increasing activism for women's rights in both America and Britain at this time in the 19th Century, no woman was mentioned in reports of the proceedings. While there may have been women in attendance, it seems clear that women were excluded from leadership when the organization was formed.

'Educate the people'

The next major American news report from a world conference of Methodism was found in 1931, when the *New York Times* published highlights of a meeting held in Atlanta, Georgia. Among the topics for the conference were "extremely rigid censorship of the theatre." Rev. Thomas Tiplady of the Wesleyan Methodist Church of Great Britain urged his cohorts, "Let us not make the mistake the Puritans made when they closed the theatres. Let us, rather, educate the people. Public opinion is the final censorship."[5]

Reverend Tiplady proved himself remarkably prescient when he predicted that within 25 years, all churches would have "motion picture apparatus" and that noted pastors would address millions via talking pictures. Given that television was already in experimental stages in the United States, with the first regular commercial broadcast by NBC in 1939, the good reverend's insight no doubt was guided by the same spirit that led John Wesley to make use of the varied media of his own day.

Still, these reports continued to show that leadership of the worldwide Methodist body remained in the hands of church men, with little or no mention of the contributions of church women.

The Great Depression, which devastated world economics in the 1930s, and the effects of World War II from 1939 to 1945 combined to interrupt meetings of the global Methodist organization for 16 years after the 1931 session. World Methodist Conferences resumed with the seventh session in October, 1947, in Springfield, Massachusetts.[6] The Springfield Conference was marked by a new awareness of the world, no doubt engendered by the experiences of World War II. The conference itself was reorganized into a world Council, composed of members recommended by their churches, which would conduct the business of the organization between the full conferences held once every five years. This reorganization, modeled after the World Council of Churches, created an executive model for management and fostered the transformation of the World Methodist Conference into a body that, through worship, speeches and workshops, served to encourage and inspire John Wesley's spiritual descendants to spread scriptural holiness around the world.

In reorganizing the Council, the Springfield delegates also eliminated the previous Anglo-Saxon bias in leadership by creating 24 regions for representation. However, while geographical concerns drew little opposition, the larger issue of racial discrimination touched off heated debate. The Rev. Edmund D. Soper of Evanston, Illinois, ignited the discussion when he read a draft of "a message to the Methodists of the world," coauthored by Soper and Dr. Harold Roberts of Surrey, England.

"We in the conference have been brought face to face with the problem of the races. In the conference itself there was no discrimination; black and white, Indian and Chinese met together with no sense of incongruity," Soper read to the assembly.

"But that condition does not extend to the cities from which many delegates came. There is no issue which is facing Methodists today more menacing than that of the race problem which has raised its ugly head so widely that it has become a world issue.

"We are all guilty before God. How can we claim to be Methodists, not to speak of being Christian, with our cherished doctrine of a universal atonement, and treat our Negro brother almost as if he were an outsider? We do not minimize the difficulties; we recognize that we are in the aftermath of the master-slave condition, and yet, with all that, we acknowledge and urge upon all our fellow Methodists to realize that this problem is pressing upon us as never before."[7]

Among the programs started by the 1947 session that continue today are the ministers' exchange; an international affairs committee that corresponds with a committee of the same name at the World Council of Churches; a youth organization; and a women's federation. Acknowledgement of the vital role of Methodist women worldwide marks the first public mention of women's leadership in major media reports on the World Methodist Conference in the modern era.[8]

After a 1951 conference in Oxford, England, the year 1956 was a watershed time for the World Methodist Council. The Ninth World Methodist Conference opened at Lake Junaluska, North Carolina, with the dedication of what *New York Times* reporter George Dugan called "one of the world's largest and finest collections of John Wesley memorabilia"[9] — the foundation of the collection that has expanded into today's World Methodist Museum.

Racism a major issue

The Ninth Conference gathered a few months after The Methodist Church in the United States approved the ordination of women as elders in full connection, following decades of women serving in pastoral positions without full ecclesiastical authority. However, racism, not sexism, continued to be the major issue for the World Methodist Council in 1956.

Despite segregation across the American South, black delegates were housed at the Lake Junaluska facilities along with white delegates. However, a disagreement arose over the swimming pool, which had been closed Sept. 1 for refurbishment. Some delegates thought the pool had been closed so that whites and blacks would not commingle, but the facility's administrators insisted the closing was an annual event. "Quiet efforts were started to bring the swimming-pool issue to the conference floor. Rain and cooler weather gave to the controversy a purely academic flavor, however, and 'cooler heads' apparently prevailed," Dugan wrote.[10]

Nonetheless, the racism issue wouldn't go away, especially as the conference was pressed to establish a single world headquarters at Lake Junaluska, rather than continue with two secretariats — one American, one British. New York attorney Charles C. Parlin led a group of dissidents who argued that the Council's secretariat should be in Geneva,

Switzerland, home of the World Council of Churches; in New York City, home of the National Council of Churches in the United States; or in London, birthplace of the Methodist movement.[11]

Parlin had other persuasive arguments. At the time, Lake Junaluska facilities — called "the crown jewel of Southern Methodism" — were open only two months out the year. Furthermore, North Carolina segregation laws would prevent black delegates, even with international status, from being admitted to the facility on a regular basis. Parlin and his supporters favored his hometown of New York City for the Council headquarters, reasoning that it would be more accessible for international delegates. The decision was deferred until the next Executive Committee a year later in Rome,[12] but the Council continued to maintain two secretariats, one American and one British, until after the American Civil Rights Act of 1964 abolished segregation. Over continued objections, the world headquarters of the Council finally was established at Lake Junaluska, where it remains today.

By the 1950s, the World Methodist Council, like its multi-denominational counterpart the World Council of Churches, was being recognized as a major force in ecumenical relations. Hopes were high during this era that the world's churches would come together around their shared beliefs and somehow foster global peace despite the shadow of the nuclear age. Messages urging the conference to take a leading role in peacemaking came to the 1956 conference from U.S. President Dwight D. Eisenhower,[13] and to the 1961 conference in Oslo, Norway, from U.S. President John F. Kennedy.[14]

Catholic spirit

World Methodist historians often note that Methodism, with its roots in the Anglican Church, is only "two steps away from the Catholic Church." Over the years, the World Methodist Council has worked to strengthen and expand those ties. The Second Ecumenical Council of the Vatican, known as Vatican II, was revolutionizing the Roman Catholic Church in the early 1960s, and the progress made at that historic consultation were felt in the World Methodist Council as well.

Bishop Fred P. Corson of the Methodist Church, then president of the Council, commended Pope Paul VI for his 1964 encyclical,

"Ecclesiam Suam," which offered the services of organized Christianity for the solution of world problems, especially those of peace, human rights and social welfare.[15] Then in July, 1966, the Catholic Church and the World Methodist Council announced the establishment of a joint committee to "explore common studies and action in a framework of Christian unity."[16] Talks between Methodists and Catholics continue today, and some of the relationships built during these dialogues were to play a role in Frances Alguire's term.

Yet for all its recognition and progress, the World Methodist Council continued to lag behind in female representation and female leadership well into the 1970s.

A breakthrough for lay leadership occurred in 1970, sadly because of the death of then-president Bishop Odd Hagen of Norway. The Council's Executive Committee elected the former leader of the anti-Junaluska forces, Wall Street attorney Charles C. Parlin of Englewood, New Jersey, as president. Parlin, at age 72, became the first lay person to head the Council, serving the unexpired remainder of Hagen's term until the 1971 Conference in Denver, Colorado.[17]

Once the barrier to lay leadership had been broken, even for a short time under expedient circumstances, greater progress became possible.

She started in Dublin

Frances Alguire journeyed into the rich fields of World Methodist Council history in 1976, when she and her husband Donald were named by Bishop Paul Washburn of Chicago, Illinois, to be delegates to the World Methodist Conference in Dublin, Ireland.

Frances left their Downers Grove, Illinois, home about a week before Donald to attend the World Federation of Methodist Women assembly prior to the World Methodist Conference. The trip marked her first solo international trek. Her first stop was Shannon, Ireland, the major debarkation point for flights from the United States. She transferred from the airport to a train, headed for Dublin, and was delighted to meet two United Methodist Women from Mississippi to share the journey. The threesome shepherded one another to Trinity College, where the World Federation met.

Don arrived a week later as the 13th World Methodist Conference began. Staying in the same bed-and-breakfast inn with them were the Rev. Donald and Bertha English, and the Rev. Kenneth and Mary Greet of the Methodist Church of Great Britain.

Their hostel may have been the site of one of the most distinguished informal gatherings of World Methodist leadership, for that year, Dr. Greet was elected Chair of the Council, and fifteen years later, Donald English would be Frances' immediate predecessor.[18]

High on the list of actions for the meeting of the 450-member World Methodist Council in Dublin was the election of a clergy member of The United Methodist Church's North Texas Annual Conference, the Rev. Joe Hale, to be the Council's third general secretary, succeeding Dr. Lee Tuttle. As with their new friends, the Englishes and the Greets, neither the Alguires nor Dr. Hale and his hospitable wife, Mary, had any inkling then how closely their lives would intertwine over the next 25 years.

Mid-week the conference participants gathered for a Peace Parade through the streets of Dublin that was marred by a bomb threat. Fire trucks came screaming to the scene, sirens blaring, but the group marched on, singing.[19]

Historic developments

The Dublin conference gave the Alguires the opportunity to participate in two other historic developments: the establishment of the World Methodist Peace Award, and the second report of groundbreaking dialogue between Methodists and Catholics.

The World Methodist Peace Award was proposed by Dr. A. Stanley Leyland of Epsom, England, in response to a stirring address by Rev. Eric Gallagher, a Methodist Church of Ireland leader who was then at the heart of the conflict between Catholic and Protestant forces in Belfast, Northern Ireland. In proposing an annual honor for a peacemaker, Leyland reminded the conference of Gallagher's suggestions about how important it would be for World Methodists to give their public support to peacemaking efforts around the globe.[20]

The Alguires were among those delegates who agreed that the first award should go to a person in Northern Ireland, but could then go to peacemakers working in other areas around the world. An award committee was set up to choose recipients. The conference chose "Courage,

Creativity, and Consistency" as the criteria for honoring a peacemaker. The first World Methodist Peace Award went to a 69-year-old trade union and peace movement activist, Sadie Patterson of Belfast. Mrs. Patterson was honored for a simple, yet profoundly significant task: trying to persuade people in Northern Ireland to stop killing each other. The acute need for peacemakers was tragically underscored when, within hours after Mrs. Patterson's award was announced, her grand-nephew was gunned down in northwest Belfast as he drove to his job.[21]

'Recognize our common heritage'

The Dublin report on Methodist-Catholic dialogue showed the infancy of the talks, as conferees were exploring a range of topics without settling on a focus, said Rev. Gillian Kingston, president of the Irish Council of Churches and Co-Chair of the Irish Inter-Church Meeting, in a 2006 report.[22] Nonetheless, Rev. Kingston noted, in Dublin the conferees were propelled by a common recognition: "More than once . . . we have been called to recognize our common heritage; not just to put an ecumenical veneer on the otherwise unalterable furniture of our separation, but to discover the underlying realities on which our churches are founded and to which the common feature of our heritage point." Since Dublin, the World Methodist Council has entered into dialogue with a number of partners — the Roman Catholic Church, the Lutheran World Federation, the World Alliance of Reformed Churches, the Anglican Communion, The Salvation Army and, in an exploratory manner, with the Ecumenical Patriarchate of Orthodox Churches.

The Dublin meeting also was noted for the election of Princess Pilo Levu Tuita of Tonga, as part of the eight-member presidium. Until his death in 2006, Tonga was ruled by the princess' father, King Taufa'ahau Tupou IV, reputed to be the only "Methodist king" in the world.[23] The report of Princess Pilo's election was one of the first, if not the first, evidence that women were beginning to share in World Methodist leadership.

These issues and more were to become intimately familiar to Frances Alguire as her own gifts for effective leadership became known to World Methodists.

In 1981, at the 14th World Methodist Conference in Hawaii, Frances and Donald Alguire witnessed the latest episode of the World Methodist

Council's longstanding efforts toward Christian unity and against racism.

That year, the Council established the World Methodist Evangelism Institute, a joint ministry of World Evangelism, the World Methodist Council and Candler School of Theology at United Methodist-related Emory University in Atlanta.[24] A major goal of the Institute was to raise up indigenous evangelists by holding training around the world. The intention of the program, from its founding by the Rev. Sir Alan Walker of Australia, was to root the Gospel within indigenous cultures, in hopes of counteracting harmful cultural influences that had occurred in previous missionary efforts.

Another step toward the unity of all Christians was acknowledged that year. The Council's ecumenical committee reported that a dialogue with U.S. Lutherans, begun in 1977, had produced a common statement recognizing the validity of one another's baptisms administered in accordance with Scripture.[25]

Meanwhile, the Council also passed its first resolution opposed to the Republic of South Africa's racial segregation system known as apartheid — a topic that would engage World Methodist leaders through the decade of the 1980s as international pressure was brought to bear on South Africa.

A beginning in 1981

His Eminence Sunday Mbang, Commander of the Order of Nigeria and prelate emeritus of the Methodist Church of Nigeria, recalled that he first became closely associated with Frances Alguire at the 1981 Conference in Honolulu. "This proved to be the beginning of a long, meaningful and most rewarding relationship," he wrote in a remembrance.[26]

"There, at that Conference, I became a member of the Executive Committee of the World Methodist Council, and so was Mrs. Alguire, who had been connected with the world body before me," Dr. Mbang wrote. "As members of this important body, our contributions to the Council were through her different committees."

Frances was assigned to the finance committee. Her new responsibilities required annual trips to Executive Committee meetings held throughout the world. By then, Frances had been accompanying Don on about every third of his international business trips, so Don relished the opportunity to be "the spouse" accompanying Frances on her trips.[27]

Five years later, Frances and Don attended the 1986 World Methodist Conference in Nairobi, Kenya, the first such conference on the African continent. In one sense, the 1986 conference brought Frances full circle, bringing her back to the city where she began her efforts to help the continent's churches and societies develop more fully.

That year Frances met Ralph C. Young, a genial churchman with long experience in international ecumenical work. Mr. Young was the Council's newly appointed deputy secretary in Geneva, Switzerland, home of several world ecumenical organizations such as the World Council of Churches, the Lutheran World Federation and the World Alliance of Reformed Churches. "Ever since we met, I have been impressed by her effective work," said Mr. Young.[28]

In 1986, Frances was elected one of eight regional presidents, presiding over the North American Section. With her election to this position, Frances' challenges of being a laywoman in leadership among World Methodists sharpened.

Eight Methodist denominations

The scope of the work was daunting. The North American section was composed of eight major Methodist denominations: three historically Black, U.S. denominations of African Methodist Episcopal, African Methodist Episcopal Zion and Christian Methodist Episcopal; the Free Methodist Church; the Methodist Church of Mexico; the United Methodist Church; the Wesleyan Church; and the United Church of Canada.

Each denomination assigned a representative, usually a bishop, to work as a vice president with the section president. So Frances Alguire, as the North American Section President found herself in titular superiority — at least as far as the World Methodist Council was concerned — to bishops from both churches and cultures where men ruled. Yet "superiority," while it may have existed in titles on paper, was never Frances Alguire's style. Instead she conducted her new duties as she always had, seeking to build consensus and work through teams that made the best uses of each person's gifts.[29] More than once, her leadership style gently persuaded bishops who were still used to ruling their respective churches by fiat.

A set of letters from March 1991 between Dr. Alguire and the Rev. Joe Hale, then general secretary of the World Methodist Council, illustrates the situation.

In one of their last meetings before the 1991 conference in Singapore, officers of the North American Section agreed to meeting in a suite at the Charlotte, North Carolina, International Airport. Eight of the 13 officers were present and faced a full agenda, topped by the question of how to reorganize the North American Section to encourage greater participation among member denominations.

Part of the tension stemmed from the dominance of Frances' own denomination, The United Methodist Church. As Council Treasurer John Harper phrased it, according to Dr. Alguire's notes, "it was necessary for the president of the North American section to be a United Methodist, because of the large contributions necessary from United Methodists and the need for denominational promotion of funds for the World Methodist Council."[30] In other words, because of the dominance of The United Methodist Church in North America, Council officials believed that the section president needed to be a person with standing and influence in the denomination, in order to serve as a primary interpreter of the Council and its needs to United Methodists.

Still racially homogenous

Furthermore, The United Methodist Church was then, as it has continued to be, significantly racially homogenous, with White people predominating in both its clergy and laity. This no doubt was a major sticking point for the historically Black Methodist churches, two of whom — the African Methodist Episcopal Church and the African Methodist Episcopal Church, Zion — came about after their founders had separated from the Methodist Church in the early 1800s because of racism.

Eventually the conversation evolved that someone moved — Dr. Alguire's notes don't say who — that henceforth only one United Methodist would be elected an officer of the North American Section, and that one office would be that of president.

Frances Alguire must have played her typical role of inclusive leader at the meeting, because a March 14 letter from Joe Hale, written the day after the Charlotte meeting, begins: "Many thanks for your splendid leadership yesterday! . . . We were strengthened by having everyone's input, particularly when it came to the lists of persons who have been

Service to World Methodism

Bp. V. Anderson First Vice-Pres. AME Church

Bp. H. Anderson AMEZ Church

Dr. Dudley CME Church

Dr. McKenna Free Methodist

Dr. Abbott Wesleyan Church

Bishop Jones UM Church

Mrs. Frances M. Alguire President, North American Section

Dr. Wilson UC Canada

Ms. Coronado Mexico

Mr. Harper Treasurer

Mrs. Alsdurf Asst. Treasurer

Joe Hale Secretary

Officers of the North American Section of the World Methodist Council who served with Frances Alguire in 1986-91.

Frances and Donald Alguire took a moment to pose with the doorman at the Hotel Sahil in Mumbai, India, during one of the World Methodist Council's officers' meetings.

Frances and Donald hosted Bishop Stanley Mogoba of the Methodist Church of Southern Africa in their home in Downers Grove, Illinois.

115

nominated [to the World Methodist Council] from the various episcopal areas of the United Methodist Church. . . . If the bishops knew these selections were made on the basis of the people they nominate, they would no doubt take our request for inclusiveness a bit more seriously. It was astonishing, really, that only one young person was nominated in the whole of the United Methodist Church."[31]

Dr. Hale added that the inclusion of young people would have to be rectified — as it had been in the past — at the World Methodist Conference itself.

Frances and Don continued to extend their longtime hospitality to others, especially traveling Methodists, during this time. Among their guests was Bishop M. Stanley Mogoba of the Methodist Church of Southern Africa, whose church, styled after the British Methodist Church, also included congregations in Zimbabwe and other countries bordering South Africa.

Bishop Mogoba had been directly involved in South Africa's struggle to throw off the shackles of its racial segregation system known as apartheid, an Afrikaans word meaning "separateness."[32] He had been imprisoned along with Nelson Mandela and other leaders of the African National Congress on the notorious Robbin Island, and suffered, along with so many other prisoners, the injuries of that experience, including beatings and torture.[33] A man small in stature but with a wide, bright smile, Dr. Mogoba was about the same height as Frances, so they could look each other directly in the eyes and see shining there the light of their common faith.

The bishop's visit was a whirlwind tour through America at a tense, delicate time. His country was just beginning a series of negotiations to dismantle apartheid, negotiations that would last for the next three years. Scheduled also to visit New York, Boston, Charlotte, Dallas and Houston, the bishop spent four days with the Alguires at their home in Downers Grove, Illinois, during the Chicago stop of his two-week trip. "I have vivid memories of the lovely time I spent in your home," Dr. Mogoba wrote in a 2002 letter, after he had been elected a member of the Parliament of the Republic of South Africa.[34]

In 1991, the World Methodist Conference held its first gathering on the Asian continent, meeting in the island nation of Singapore at the tip of Malaysia near the equator.

The Rev. Hal Brady, who at the time was senior pastor of First United Methodist Church in Dallas, Texas, remembers the trip well.

"My wife and I were flying to Singapore for our initial experience with the World Methodist Council and Conference," Dr. Brady said. "As soon as we got to the crowded middle section of five seats in the back of the plane and got settled, we introduced ourselves to none other than Don and Fran Alguire. Immediately, they took us under their wings and we have stayed there ever since.

"Throughout the Singapore Conference, Fran made us feel very welcomed and included. She made it a point to introduce us to every one she knew (which is quite a lot of people). So from the beginning of our experience with World Methodism, we felt a keen friendship and acceptance. And it was Fran who was responsible for my getting more involved with the Council."[35]

Presidium members

In 1991, at the 16th World Methodist Conference in Singapore, Fran was elected an officer of the Council, along with her colleague, His Eminence Sunday Mbang of Nigeria.

"The whole situation changed for the better in 1991, at the Singapore Conference," Dr. Mbang wrote in a remembrance. "At that Conference both of us were elected members of the Presidium of the World Methodist Council with our amiable, dynamic and brilliant Dr. Donald English as the Chair of the Council for the next five years. The late Dr. English was not only our leader and an outstanding Church administrator, pastor, academician and evangelist, he was above all our friend. It was an unusual privilege for both of us to have had five years very close and fruitful relationship with the revered clergyman, who helped to radically influence and positively change our outlook to life."[36]

A year later, after communism had fallen, the Alguires traveled to the resort town of Varna, Bulgaria, on the Black Sea, for the 1992 Executive Committee meeting. The meeting had its own set of historic moments:

* The reclamation from the Bulgarian government of a building that was originally a Methodist church, but had been used by the communist government for decades as a theater;

* The groundbreaking of a new multi-story Methodist center;

* The presentation of the World Methodist Peace Award to the Rev. Zdravko Beslov, a survivor of horrendous imprisonment by the Bulgarian government who had kept the Methodist Church secretly alive

in his country throughout the communist era.

Then came the 1996 World Methodist Conference in Rio de Janeiro, Brazil, the first time global Methodists gathered in South America.

Emotions were running high at the World Methodist Council meeting prior to the conference as names were put forth to succeed the Rev. Donald English of the Methodist Church of Great Britain as Chair.

Mary Um, General Secretary of the Board of Social Responsibility & Laity of the Korean Methodist Church and a member of Honorary Order of Jerusalem, described the nominating process.

'The atmosphere was tense'

"I will not forget a meeting held in Cambridge England in October 1995, when the WMC Nominating Committee met.," Ms. Um wrote in a remembrance.[37] "The atmosphere in the committee was so tense as its job was to nominate the next WMC chairperson. Powerful male church leaders aspired to the position. The vice-chairperson who was chairing the meeting was a woman from Australia. We were all challenged to find among the candidates who was the most conversant with the WMC activities. At that meeting the current chairperson, Dr. Donald English, asked me a question, "because many English-speaking persons dominated the discussions, what do you suggest?" I answered, "Why don't we consider Dr. Frances Alguire for the next chairperson?" To my surprise almost everyone shouted out "Yes, I agree with Mary Um!" It surprised me that most members had Frances Alguire in their minds. Then Dr. English declared that Dr. Frances Alguire was nominated to be the next WMC chairperson."

Even with that show of support among Nominating Committee members, the jockeying for election among clergy at the conference was intense, Frances remembered.[38] An Asian clergyman promised to raise a million dollars for the Council if he were elected chairman. Another clergyman from North America quizzed Frances sharply on her theological beliefs.

"I simply told him that I preferred to focus on the things that unite us, rather than what divides us," she said.[39]

Another stumbling block emerged before they arrived in Brazil, however. The Nominating Committee, in asking to put Frances up for election, told her that the World Methodist Council had no budget to pay the expenses of a layperson to be Chair, since those costs were typically borne by the chairman's own church (and to date all chairs had been men). She and Don took counsel with their family, and they decided to make the expenses of Frances' term part of their charitable donation to the world church, on top of maintaining their considerable financial contributions to their local congregation in New Buffalo, Michigan.

"We told the family, 'We're spending your inheritance,' " Don laughed.[40]

Frances' family also was aware that she felt anxiety about her ability to preside over the World Methodist Council. Not only was she a layperson and a woman, but she had not served as vice Chair of the Council, a traditionally expected role of preparation. Her daughter Mary's husband, Robert Papish, wrote the following poem to encourage his mother-in-law.[41]

ODE TO WOMEN
There is a reason,
That Christ was born of woman,
And lived on earth: Child, Youth, Man,
Dying in the fullness of maturity.
He lived not just the pain and limits
Of human nature,
But also the human love of His mother.
Selfless, invested in the Child,
Redeemed by love, in turn.

That love speaks in a quiet voice,
A voice that can't be heard above the tumult
And the shouting of the strife of men.
It cannot be heard when women walk behind,
Instead of alongside.

It cannot be heard when we turn aside
From the tasks of love.
It reminds us of chores undone.
It cautions us to remain true, to cleave;
Crafters to the work unfinished.

It is past time for those,
Who have suffered the pain of childbirth,
To stand before the multitude,
Bidden only by love,
And remind us all that there is work
That has been reserved for us . . .
To redeem the promise, born in pain,
And pain again revisited.

Bolstered by her family and her faith, Frances shook off the election pressure and became content to accept any outcome. "I didn't feel any competition; the decision was up to the 500 delegates who voted," she said.[42]

When the final vote was tallied, Frances M. Alguire had stepped firmly into history as the first laywoman to be elected Chair of the World Methodist Council.

Reaching out

According to her longtime friend Vivian Miner, Frances' first acts at the Rio de Janeiro conference were to approach those clergy who had resisted her nomination and invite them to serve with her in leadership. Another longtime friend, Jean Beal of Rockford, Illinois, who had served as Northern Illinois Conference vice president with Frances, also remembered her peacemaking effort.

"I shall never forget when she was being elected as president of the Methodist World Council, knowing that a certain clergyman felt he should rightfully be the one elected, she affirmed him and included him in the work of the Council," Mrs. Beal wrote in a remembrance. "Knowing I would have reacted in a different way, I was humbled to realize that Fran had an understanding of faith that I had yet to achieve."[43]

Among the clergy who were delighted by Frances' election was Rev. Hal Brady, by now senior pastor at St. Luke's United Methodist Church in Columbus, Georgia.

"When Fran became the first woman president of the Council, I was asked to Chair the Program Committee for the 2001 World Methodist Conference that was held in Brighton, England," Dr. Brady said. "With that responsibility, I had opportunity to work closely with Fran for the next five years as we prepared for that Conference. I found Fran to be a great leader with a heart for inclusiveness. She always put others and their needs first. Her ability to listen is phenomenal."[44]

The Council's Geneva Secretary, Ralph Young, remembered being moved by Frances' first address.

"She challenged those present: 'Each of our lives has a ripple effect, which can make a difference to many . . . We are called to become activists for peace, justice and mercy, sharing the light and love of Christ

Jesus into the twenty-first century."[45]

"During the next five years, wherever she traveled all over the world, Dr. Alguire was consistent in practicing what she had preached," Young said.

Dr. Denis C. Dutton, a past bishop of the Methodist Church of Malaysia, also verified Frances Alguire's inclusive leadership.

"I cannot remember when I first met Frances Alguire," he wrote in a remembrance.[46] "However, whenever it was, my earliest recollection is that she was always with her husband, Don. Wherever you found one the other would be close at hand, and this impressed me very much. I can still visualize their smiling faces. This is the other thing about them that is etched in my mind. It was not until Fran became the President of the World Methodist Council, did I fully realize how committed they were to the idea of Methodist ecumenism.

"While she was president, I came to know Fran better and admired her qualities of leadership that are seldom seen today. She is a very focused person. She did not make decisions on the basis of what was politically correct but on the basis of what was right, on what the World Methodist Council stood for. She often spoke her mind in the most gentle way that did not give offense to anyone. However, you could detect her firmness whenever it was a matter of principle that was involved. Her goals were clear and she pursued them with a fierceness that was not hard to detect. At the same time she was always willing for differing views to be expressed. She had the art of making people comfortable when debate became heated."

Struggling to improve

The 17th World Methodist Conference in Rio de Janeiro marked a sea of change, not only in the election of Frances Alguire, but in coming to grips with crucial needs. As the Rev. Ronald P. Patterson, then publisher of the *United Methodist Reporter*, observed in an Aug. 22, 1996, column:

> Since its inception, the World Methodist Conference has opened windows of understanding to the world, the global church and addressed challenges Christians face in faith, mission and witness.
>
> As the Conference, and its 500-member governing body, move into the 21st century, it will need to deal with some weighty

121

issues if its is to be a viable movement for the future. Some of these are:

- Attracting more youths and people in their 30s and 40s;
- Overcoming the perceived white-male-dominated leadership;
- Seeking out more women for key leadership and program responsibilities;
- Overcoming a perception of paternalism;
- Striving to be more culturally inclusive in all aspects of its life and witness.

. . . The election of Frances M. Alguire as Chair of the World Methodist Council signals a giant step in this direction.[47]

Despite the hopeful note sounded by Dr. Patterson and others, Frances Alguire still faced prejudice from both men and women who resisted her standing as a laywoman in church leadership.

Several male World Methodist Council members, often from cultures that restricted women's roles, were uncomfortable approaching Frances. Instead, they approached her husband. "I finally told them, 'I'm not even on your committee; go see your boss,'" Donald Alguire said.[48]

Catherine Alguire also remembers her mother discussing some of the challenges of being a trail-blazing women leader.

"When first elected as the President of World Methodism, Mom told us of being asked on several occasions how she could possibly feel comfortable being the leader of a group of only men — who were sometimes quite outspoken and competitive," Catherine and her sister Mary wrote in a remembrance. "We laughed and reminded her of her several decades of training with Dad. While both of them are a strong individual and independent in their own right, they have a steadfast loyalty in supporting each other."[49]

Sometimes prejudice reared its head from unlikely sources.

For instance, in 1999, Frances attended a celebration honoring a longtime World Methodist Council leader, the Rev. William K. Quick, upon his retirement from Metropolitan United Methodist Church in Detroit, Michigan, where he had served since 1975. During a reception after the ceremony at which Frances spoke, she was approached by a clergyman's spouse. "You're a small person for such a big job," she said. Although taken aback by the woman's words, Frances replied genially: "I'm the same size as John Wesley."[50]

By this time, Frances had gained academic accreditation commensurate with her lifelong learning, thanks to two United Methodist-related institutions, Adrian College in her home state of Michigan and Garrett-Evangelical Theological Seminary, which in June 1997 bestowed honorary doctorates on her in recognition of her contributions to World Methodism. The Garrett-Evangelical Theological Seminary citation conveying a doctor of humane letters degree read in part: " . . . you have devoted your life to Christian service. You blend in your own ministry the qualities of evangelical commitment, critical and creative reason, and prophetic participation in society."[51] Years later, her daughter Mary would remind her mother that long before she received her doctorates, Frances Alguire had earned not only her nursing degree but an "LBD" — "Learning By Doing," the same kind of life experience "degree" earned by her devoted mother, Mary Werner.

The ministry of all baptized

Even though her new status as a learned doctor of the church conveyed greater formal standing, Frances chose to appear not in ecclesiastical garb, but in layperson's clothing. "I was representing the ministry of all who are baptized," she said.[52] Yet even when wearing her most formal outfit, a sumptuous navy velvet dress that set off the ornate badge of office she wore as Council Chair, Frances would sometimes be confronted by church officials who felt she didn't belong.

In early January 2000, she was chosen to read Scripture at the opening of the Holy Door at St. Paul's-Outside-the-Walls to usher in The Catholic Church's Jubilee Year in preparation for the third millennium since the birth of Jesus Christ. Following Pope John Paul II, Ecumenical Patriarch Bartholomew II and other dignitaries, Frances was the sole woman in the procession into the chapel. Unexpectedly, since she had been invited to the ceremony, she was stopped at the door by one of the Vatican's imposing Swiss Guards. Thinking quickly, she was able to get the sentinel to admit her by pointing to her World Methodist Council badge of office.[53]

After the ceremony, Frances shook hands with all the prelates on the dais, including a warm, intimate greeting from Pope John Paul II. Her participation in the ceremony startled many of the clerics there, but at least one person was thrilled by her presence. Outside the chapel after the service, Frances was hugged enthusiastically by an Italian nun, who told her: "You must be very brave!" [54]

Courage was needed during Frances Alguire's term. The state of the World Methodist Council's finances had deeply concerned her from the start. Her anxiety stemmed from the realization that issue of a lack of budget for the world chairperson's expenses would likely keep other capable laymen and laywomen from serving in the future. However, Frances quickly recognized that the larger issue was the continued financial health of the World Methodist Council, since many of its members in developing countries, often burdened by international debt, were finding themselves unable to pay their proportionate share of the Council's expenses.

Endowment campaign

Not long after her election, Frances proposed to the Council's Presidium that they undertake an endowment campaign. Finance Chair Donald Fites, president of the Caterpillar Corporation headquartered in Peoria, Illinois, surprised even Frances when he set a high target: $20 million.[55] The endowment was among the priorities for the Executive Committee to consider when it met in September 1997 in Rome.

Nearly 200 people had arrived at the Domus Marie Catholic Retreat Center on Rome's Appia Antica when Frances received a telephone call from Dr. Joe Hale, the Council's General Secretary. His wife, Mary, who had suffered a life-threatening stroke the previous year, had tumbled from her wheelchair en route to changing planes in Newark, New Jersey. The fall fractured her leg, and for the first time in his tenure, Dr. Hale had to be excused from a meeting he had arranged.

Ralph Young, who took over some of the administrative support, remembered that Frances faced the emergency with her gift for calling on each individual's best talents.

"She immediately assured Joe that she would be in touch with him daily by telephone, and that she would have meetings with the other officers at breakfast every day, confident they would be ready to help," Dr. Young said.[56]

Linda Greene, who was Dr. Hale's administrative assistant at the time, also remembers how Dr. Alguire rose to the challenge of conducting her first Executive Committee meeting without the Council's supremely capable, longtime general secretary.

"We learned that Dr. Hale had sent the materials he was carrying to Rome with Mrs. Hale's caregiver, Mrs. Rosalind Buchanan," Ms. Greene recalled.[57] "As word spread about the accident, and the fact that Dr. and Mrs. Hale would not be able to travel on to Rome, Executive Committee members, support staff, even the Italian Methodists, all came to say they were immediately going to pray for the Hales and to pray for our staff as we carried on the meeting.

"The Italian Methodists spent many hours at the retreat center in order to help us in any way they could. The retreat center had a bank of pay phones. My first priority was to locate Dr. and Mrs. Hale at a hospital near the Newark Airport. I did not speak Italian, I had no Italian coins, I did not know how to use the phone, I did not know the name of the hospital. The Italian young people handled the first part until I could speak with an American directory assistance operator who steered me in the right direction. After only two tries, I located Dr. Hale."

Ms. Greene recalled that in addition to the unprecedented focus on Council finances, the agenda was filled with urgent and important activities. There were plans to be made for ushering in the new millennium marking the 2,000th anniversary of the birth of Jesus Christ. The Executive Committee and their spouses, along with other church observers, were to attend the presentation of the 1997 World Methodist Peace Award to the Community of Sant'Egidio in Trastevere, one of Rome's oldest neighborhoods. One evening was allocated to a presentation by the Italian Methodist Church in the magnificent green marble chapel at Domus Marie. The entire group was scheduled to meet Pope John Paul II, a meeting arranged by Cardinal Walter Cassidy, head of the Vatican's Council on ecumenical relations, and Monsignor Tim Galligan, liaison representative to the World Methodist Council from the Vatican.

A community of peace

The presentation of the World Methodist Peace Award to the Community of Sant'Egidio was another inspiration of Frances Alguire's leadership, for it marked the first time that an entire organization of peacemakers was honored.

Dr. Monica Attias of Rome, Italy, a Sant'Egidio member, recalled the development of the organization's relationship with Dr. Alguire:

"When I first met Dr Frances Alguire, she had just taken her position as President of the World Methodist Council. She came to Rome to participate in an International Meeting of Prayer for Peace organized by the Community of Sant'Egidio, 'Peace is the name of God.' On that occasion, representing World Methodism among many male leaders of the great world religions, she was trying to 'invent' a new role as first laywoman in an inter-religious context. Her warmth and humanity have been the best way to gain respect and love by the representatives of other religious traditions.

"Frances' sense of friendship as an important dimension of her faith is what has most impressed the members of the Community of Sant'Egidio and me personally. During the conferences we have often spent time together, going beyond institutional relationships and establishing spiritual links that are still lasting. She has become a faithful guest of the Sant'Egidio meetings and an active support in many initiatives, especially against the death penalty in the world. In the year 2000, Frances Alguire signed a 'Global Petition to put Pressure on the U.S. to Abolish the Death Penalty.' With her other religious and political leaders signed as the Dalai Lama; the Indonesian president, Abdurrahman Wahid; the Archbishop of Canterbury, George Carey.

"Through her, the WMC learned to know Sant'Egidio closely and decided to give it the 1997 World Methodist Peace Award."[58]

When the Executive Committee and others gathered at a Trastevere church for the ceremony, Frances invested Dr. Andrea Riccardi, one of the Community's founders, with the peace medal on behalf of all the members of the Sant'Egidio community while Italian television recorded the historic event.

Meeting Pope John Paul II

Initially there was to have been a private audience with the pontiff, but the event was cancelled because of Pope John Paul's frail health. Instead, the World Methodist group was seated on the portico of St. Peter's Basilica during the pope's weekly audience addressing thousands in St. Peter's Square.

"Just after he spoke, Fran was introduced to the pope and had thoughtfully taken him a gift, a bound, gold-leafed copy of our World Methodist Council Museum booklet, which she presented to him," Ms. Greene said. "During his address Pope John Paul II recognized the World Methodist group and prayed for Dr. and Mrs. Hale during his prayers concluding the event. He then turned to our group to meet and visit with the World Methodist Council delegation." [59]

Mary Ellen Bullard of Montgomery, Alabama, a member of the Executive Committee, had vivid memories of the event:

"An audience of around 20,000 was gathered in St. Peter's Square. The members of the Executive Committee were seated on a platform a few feet away from Pope John Paul II from where he addressed the audience.

"At this occasion, Dr. Alguire was the personification of dignity dressed in a navy blue velvet dress with an impressive matching hat. She led us to our seats and as we looked over the audience we saw Pope John Paul II riding in his white specially-built car called the 'popemobile' through the many aisles, greeting all the people until he was driven up a red carpet to his special golden chair on the platform. We were almost close enough to touch him.

". . . After greeting special visitors, he moved to the World Methodist Council delegation for personal greetings. Though he was weak due to failing health, he stood and with enthusiasm visited with those present. I will never forget how attentive and supportive Dr. Alguire was to him. They had a warm and amiable relationship. He held her hand to steady himself as he stood greeting individuals in the group."[60]

Mrs. Bullard said that one of her treasured mementoes from the occasion is a large close-up photograph showing Pope John Paul II and Dr. Frances Alguire surrounded by the leaders of World Methodism: Bishop Lawi Imathiu of Kenya; Dr. John Barrett and Dr. Donald English of England; Dr. Eddie Fox, Dr. Maxie Dunnam and Bishop Donald Ming of the USA; Bishop Sundo Kim of South Korea; His Eminence Sunday Mbang of Nigeria; and Dr. Olav Parnamets of Estonia.

Many invitations

In Linda Greene's estimation, the World Methodist Council's 1997 week in Rome, meeting Pope John Paul II and other Roman Catholic leaders, resulted in many invitations for Dr. Alguire to represent World Methodism at many global events sponsored by the church or by Pope John Paul II during her term. "I sensed the delight and genuine friendship extended to Fran and Don Alguire, and it was a plus for the World Methodist Council that they were able to be present at the annual Day of Prayer for Peace in Assisi (several times) and other major Roman Catholic-sponsored events. It often appeared that Fran was the only woman on the platform at some of these events!" Ms. Green said.

One of the talents that Frances Alguire used to conduct her crucial first Executive Committee meeting was her gift for bringing people together.

The Domus Marie retreat center has one central dining room, so Executive Committee members had opportunity to get acquainted as they shared meals. "Fran Alguire is a people person, so she and Don enjoyed dining with different people and groups, and this seemed to be very much appreciated," Linda Greene said.[61] "People hesitate to speak with World Methodist Council leaders during meal times, as many times they are having lunch meetings or, in the evening, preparing for the next day. Fran's friendliness and her willingness to share meals with the group made her seem much more 'approachable' and people seemed much more open to talk with her."

Subtle techniques

Ms. Greene recalled that Dr. Alguire also had a few subtle techniques for keeping the meeting on track and in order.

"Instead of calling the Executive Committee session to order in a demanding or authoritarian manner, she quietly opened the meetings by lighting a candle followed by a short devotional and prayer," Ms. Green said.

"Instead of spending valuable time debating procedural matters, she appointed a very experienced and trusted person as parliamentarian at the beginning of the week. The World Methodist Council has its own approved Rules of Debate, but in a group this size, coming from so many countries and denominations, almost everyone has some difference in following rules, interpretations, etc., so procedure could evolve into a major debate if not controlled. Dr. Alguire followed agenda items, allowing ample time for presentation and debate, then voting. She has the gift of being direct and keeping the group focused on the item at hand, but also sensitivity to those who wish to be heard."[62]

His Eminence Sunday Mbang of Nigeria also noted Frances' humility in leadership. "Mrs. Alguire never believed in a one-man and one-woman show. She is not an all-knowing and all-sufficient super woman. Her style of leadership was corporate. She believes in wide consultation. She has always a listening ear. Despite her experience in many areas of our life, she is always ready and willing to learn."[63]

Early in the week in Rome, Dr. Alguire added an element that further brought the group together, Ms. Greene recalled. Time had been allocated throughout the week for standing committees or groups to meet while in Rome. On one of these nights, Frances asked Mrs. Edith Ming, an accomplished musician and wife of Bishop Donald K. Ming of the African Methodist Episcopal Church, to coordinate the first "World Methodist Council Talent Show."

Those in attendance were surprised and entertained to see leading Methodist bishops, pastors, lay people and their spouses display hidden talents. Bishop Nathaniel Linsey of the Christian Methodist Episcopal Church led the bishops and heads of churches in singing and dancing to "Father Abraham." Dr. Bruce Robbins, then general secretary of the United Methodist General Commission on Christian Unity and Interreligious Concerns, and his wife shared their love of shaped note singing. An "Appalachian gospel" quartet included Bishop Richard Looney of Macon, Georgia; Dr. H. Eddie Fox, director of World Methodist Evangelism; Dr. George Morris, founding director of the World Methodist Evangelism Institute; and Dr. William Quick, the senior pastor of Metropolitan United Methodist Church in Detroit, Michigan. Dr. Morris followed the "gospel sing" with an "Appalachian" sermon.

Not to be outdone, the Italian Methodists reciprocated with their own charming program a few nights later. The vivid green marble columns of Domus Marie's chapel, dedicated to the Virgin Mary, seemed a perfect backdrop for learning about Italian Methodists' leaders and many projects, supplemented with music by church youth groups. The gathering responded with delighted applause when the Italian Methodists, saying they were going to sing their country's "national anthem," broke into a rousing chorus of the popular ballad, "O Sole Mio."

Near the end of that week, a small group of spouses and others not participating in Executive Committee proceedings traveled to Assisi and toured the St. Francis of Assisi grounds and building. The next morning there was a strong earthquake in Assisi, and the tremors were felt by many in the Domus Marie auditorium where the Executive Committee was meeting. Along with the World Methodist tour group, some of the hotel staff had family and friends in Assisi, so everyone anxiously checked incoming news reports. Although the chapel of St. Francis had been damaged, the tour group returned safely and no casualties were reported among the friendly hotel staff's acquaintances.

"This meeting in Rome brought the Executive Committee together in a way I had not ever seen before," wrote Linda Greene in a remembrance. "The group had prayed together, dined and visited together, lingered after meetings to speak with a new friend or continue a conversation, and seemed genuinely interested in each other and in sharing concerns. After the Talent Show, I realized that laughing, singing, and dancing together was the perfect complement to the serious nature of the business sessions, the earnest prayers for the Hales and for the meeting to go well. Many of those attending remarked it was the best Executive Committee meeting ever!"[64]

'Methodism's ambassador'

Any doubts about Frances Alguire's ability to lead the World Methodist Council were soundly dashed after her extraordinary performance at the Rome meeting of the Executive Committee.

The Rev. William K. Quick, pastor emeritus of Metropolitan United Methodist Church in Detroit, Michigan, and a visiting professor at Duke University Divinity School in Durham, North Carolina, attested to the significance of Frances Alguire's leadership. Dr. Quick was first appointed to the World Methodist Council in 1966, and served in various capacities for the next 40 years, including 30 years as a member of the Executive Committee and five years as associate general secretary for "Achieving the Vision," the capital funds endowment campaign begun at that historic Rome meeting.

"When I think of Fran, as so many of us affectionately know her, there is no term which better describes her years as the head of the World Methodist Council than to say that she was truly Methodism's ambassador to the world," Dr. Quick wrote in a remembrance.[65]

"I first encountered Fran through the North Central Jurisdictional and General Conferences. Hers was a respected voice in the highest circles of the church before she was elevated to the presidency of the Council.

"I believe Dr. Alguire presided over a quinquennium [five-year term] in which her presence and leadership was felt as perhaps no other leadership. One the reasons, of course, was the tremendously resourceful husband and companion, Donald Alguire, who helped to make it possible for his energetic, enthusiastic wife to fulfill the many requests which came constantly from a globally-growing Wesleyan family. He travelled with her at his own expense, enabling Dr. Alguire to represent the Council on every continent in every imaginable setting.

"Her relational skills, winsome personality, and contagious faith brought a witness to hundreds of thousands in the Wesleyan family and she became probably the best known voice, apart from our longtime general secretary, Dr. Joe Hale, throughout the world. A woman of deep faith and personal integrity, she takes her place alongside Susanna Wesley and Barbara Heck as a pioneer who found a special place in Methodist history."

Philippines centennial

In October 1997, Frances received an invitation from United Methodist Bishop Emerito P. Nacpil of Manila, inviting her to attend the centennial of Methodism in March 1998.[66] Glad to return to the Philippines, she agreed to commit a week to visiting the country. She brought greetings from the World Methodist family to the thousands attending the National Thanksgiving Service on March 14, 1998, and later found herself being greeted by Philippines President Fidel V. Ramos. Once again, Frances visited widely around her host country, touring United Methodist missions and ministries.

Before she went to the Philippines that year, however, a major decision was made to hold the 2001 World Methodist Conference in Brighton, England. After the invitation to come to Britain had been extended and accepted at the 1996 conference in Rio de Janeiro, a group composed of Joe Hale, Frances Alguire, and Bill Haire and Ed Seabough of Travelink, the World Methodist Council's travel agency, visited four cities in England before selecting Brighton. Later along with Dr. Hal Brady, program chair for the 2001 conference, Dr. Alguire toured the proposed Brighton site in the company of her longtime convention colleague DeWayne Woodring and Edith Ming, the program committee's secretary in late 1997. The seaside location, a favorite holiday spot for Britishers, promised to provide a welcoming venue and the site selection committee was pleased to recommend it. Their recommendation was approved by the Executive Committee and announced in the first 1998 issue of "World Parish," the Council's newsletter.[67]

Peacemaking

One of the outcomes from the 1997 Executive Committee meeting in Rome was a resolution urging the world's nations to do all they could to bring about peace in the Middle East, an effort in which Dr. Joe Hale, general secretary, had played a personal role for two decades. By November 1997, Frances signed and sent a series of letters to heads of state conveying the committee's resolution.

One of the few formal responses she received came from a representative of British Prime Minister Tony Blair. Jim Irvins of the Near East and North Africa Department of the British Foreign Office thanked Dr. Alguire for her letter, adding, "If I may say so, we find the resolution admirably balanced."[68]

Irvins continued that "the British Government is fully and actively committed to the search for a just and lasting peace in the Middle East, and to promoting the development of Palestinian areas through our aid programme. ... Minister have said they are determined that Britain should play a leading role in the search for a peace settlement that will give lasting security for Israel and justice for the Palestinians."

Frances followed up the Executive Committee's resolution with an appeal of her own in the January-February 1998 issue of "World Parish." Her words are as relevant today as when they first were published.

An Appeal: Statement from Dr. Frances M. Alguire, Chairperson of the World Methodist Council

For the past two years, I have participated in an International Meeting for Peace. Members of the Community of St. Egidio in Rome invite participants from many countries representing various religions and political positions. For three days hundreds of persons met in plenary sessions, participated in panel discussions and small group encounters. PEACE was the central theme. Peace dialogues can occur!

The World Methodist Council, representing 34 million members, has recognized persons throughout the world, who by their courage, creativity and consistency, make exceptional contributions to the cause of reconciliation and peace.

I ask, "Why do political leaders continue to think that warfaring, military force and weaponry are the way to solve problems? The fallout from war is destruction of human lives and God's creation, plus perpetuation of hatred and greed.

On behalf of a global Methodist family, I plead for the United States and Iraqi governments to weigh the human factors and seek solutions that respect the dignity of men, women, and children and families on both sides, before preemptive strikes are ordered, for they will only cause increased hostility and division in the area. Not only will the people of the countries involved suffer, but other "neighbors," who stand to suffer in the Middle East, are not only Jews living in Tel Aviv, but also Christian Palestinians living in Bethlehem and Jerusalem. Others to be considered are Muslims and Christians living in the West Bank, Syria, Jordan and Egypt. We pray for peace and justice for all of God's family.

Political leaders, when will you heed our plea?[69]

Frances underscored her peacemaking work again in November 1998, when she and Joe Hale traveled to the United Nations in New York City to present the 1998 World Methodist Peace Award to UN General Secretary Kofi Annan. In his acceptance remarks, Dr. Annan recalled his primary school education at Mfantsipim School, a Methodist institution in his native Ghana.

"There I was privileged to have teachers who understood the value of knowledge infused with moral purpose," he said. "They knew that learning and education are the strongest bulwarks against evil and ignorance. And they taught me, in the spirit of faith, that suffering anywhere concerns people everywhere, and that the light of one candle can truly illuminate the world."[70]

Ambassador to youth

As Dr. William Quick wrote, Frances Alguire, always accompanied by her faithful husband Don, continued to serve as Methodism's ambassador throughout 1998. Her travels that year included a number of surprising "firsts."

Ironically, considering her past service in support of Methodist history in America, it wasn't until August 1998 that she paid her first visit to Epworth by the Sea, the site on St. Simons Island, Georgia, that commemorates the 1735 missionary visit of John and Charles Wesley. Greeting the 6th International Christian Youth Conference on Evangelism, she reminded the travel-weary youths that it took the Wesley brothers 57 days to travel in a small sailing ship from England to the colony of Georgia, where their family's friend, Gen. James Oglethorpe, was royal governor.

Then she surprised her young audience with a bit of her own history.

"People often ask me, 'How did a non-clergy woman, living in the small village of New Buffalo, Michigan, get to be the chairperson of the World Methodist Council?' Sometimes I wonder, too, but my answer to them is, 'I said Yes.'

"The first 'Yes' was to become a follower of Jesus Christ. Other 'yeses' have been ... 'yes' to teaching Sunday School; 'yes' to serving my church locally, at conferences and within communities, nationally and globally ... and then after times of prayer and meditation, 'yes' to this position.

". . . This medallion which I am wearing will be passed to my successor in the year 2001, when my term of office is completed. It has a cross, an open Bible, seashells representing the Wesley coat of arms, and inscribed around the edges [are] the words 'Methodists are one people in all the world.' I share this with you because at some future time, perhaps one of you may be wearing this same medal as a reminder of service to World Methodism."[71]

Renewed acquaintance

While at the ICYC conference, Frances renewed her acquaintance with another young person on whom she'd had enormous influence, Esther Jadhav. The two had met in Mumbai, India, during a WMC Executive Committee. As Ms. Jadhav tells it:

"Frances Alguire came to my house for a reception being held for the confirmation service that had just taken place for my brother Emmanuel and me. My encounter with her is very clear and fresh in my mind even though it was about 10 years ago for about half a day. Frances and Donald Alguire had come to Mumbai, India for the World Methodist Council meeting and it so happened that my father and mother were responsible for taking a few of the World Methodist Council members around to some churches in their spare time, and when they came to my church Emmanuel my brother and I were scheduled to be confirmed on that Sunday.

"Frances has a smile that can light up the whole room; she has a very kind presence which is adorned with a very gracious heart. To be honest I was so impressed with the fact that she was the president of the World Methodist Council, it has always been my dream to aspire the higher heights and when I first saw her I realized that such things were possible because I could see in her eyes that she heavily relied on God to be her source of wisdom and strength. The next time I saw Fran was at St. Simon's Island at ICYC in 1998, I didn't think she would remember me with the numerous persons that she meets and to my pleasant surprise she remembered exactly who I was and in fact handed me a bracelet off her wrist to remind me of God's love and faithfulness as she encouraged me on.

"I continue to enjoy this pleasant and powerful woman of God we have in Fran and I hope that her life and her stories will be an inspiration to us all."[72]

Barely a month later, in September 1998, against a backdrop of hope for peace and unity, Frances had another encounter with a Methodist youth under tragic circumstances.

She was invited to represent World Methodist at the 12th International Meeting of People and Religions in Bucharest, Romania. Against a backdrop of worldwide unrest, including bombings and armed conflict, the event drew Christians, Muslims, Jews and other believers. Once again, the peacemaking Community of Sant'Egidio, served as host for the conference, which bore the theme "Peace is the Name of God: God, Mankind and Peoples."

A United Methodist News Service story by Linda Bloom registered the familiar themes of laypeople and women in leadership. In an interview, Dr. Alguire said that her participation had showed leaders in the Catholic and Orthodox traditions, which do not ordain women that "Methodists believe in women assuming leadership roles."[73]

"At least I'm paving the way so that future ordained women will be accepted," she was quoted by UMNS. "They'll know that women can participate and women can lead."

Frances also lifted up the crucial role of ecumenism – the ongoing quest for unity among the splintered branches of Christ's followers – in peacemaking.

"The kingdom of God is in our midst: our neighbors are all of humankind," Frances told Linda Bloom. "Our measure of success is when the ecumenical spirit of unity becomes universal and each human is provided an opportunity to participate in life to the fullest."

Yet while the conference participants discussed and pondered how religion could play a peacemaking role in the world, one person came to the gathering seeking pastoral comfort.

A United Methodist teen-ager from Texas was killed in a car accident while en route to the Bucharest airport. Unable to come to Romania for their son, and unable to bring his body home, his mother contacted the young man's hosts and asked that a Methodist be found who could conduct a memorial service for him in his own faith tradition.

She found help

Frances searched among her colleagues at the conference and found an Anglican from California who introduced her to a Romanian Catholic priest, a friend of his. At the last moment, an Orthodox priest came in. Frances asked him to translate for her. "So there we were, a Catholic, an Orthodox and a United Methodist, holding a memorial service in an Orthodox church for a young Methodist man who had died before his time."

As a layperson, Frances was not authorized to conduct the clerical functions of a Christian service of burial. Instead, she wrote a prayer that encapsulated both her faith as a Christian, and her empathy for his family.

"To you, O Lord, we lift up the soul of [our departed brother]. We do not know why he was called to his heavenly home in this sudden tragic way, but you, O Lord, are our light and our salvation. Your steadfast love and abiding presence endure forever.

"We pray for comfort for the family and friends of him as they grieve his death. Thank you for your promise to comfort those who mourn. Help us to reach out to others during this time of bereavement, as we share their burdens and together reflect on memories of him.

"God, we know that 'neither death, nor life, nor angels, nor rulers, nor things present, nor things to come, nor height, nor depth, nor anything else in all creation will be able to separate us from the love of God in Christ. (Romans 8: 38-39).

"Thank you for the gifts and graces that he shared freely while he was in our midst. We pray for your guidance as he enters his eternal home to be with Jesus. In the name of Christ we pray, Amen."[74]

Frances called the young man's bereaved parents in Texas when she returned to the United States. Reflecting later on the episode, she remarked, "I think it was the first time any such service had ever happened in Romania. And I know that God was at work."[75]

Upon her return from Bucharest, Frances spoke again of peace to another group of young people, presenting the message at the Sept. 24, 1998 chapel service at Adrian College. "Though we are all different from one another, we are all children of the same God. We are called to develop mutual friendships, characterized by genuine love and selflessness, that allows us to know one another and to acknowledge our differences, and yet accept one another. As we work with others in unity, the spirit of PEACE and understanding will grow and spread."[76]

Meeting in Jerusalem

After 18 months of advocating peace for the Middle East, Frances Alguire, Joe Hale and other officers of the World Methodist Council decided it was time to embody a physical presence in the Middle East -- to put themselves personally on the line on behalf of peacemaking, the kind of risk that Christian leaders are called upon to make as disciples of Jesus Christ.

They scheduled their Dec. 4-9, 1998 officers' meeting in Jerusalem, choosing to stay at a church-related facility in the Arab Quarter of the city. While there, they met in the Chapter House of the Cathedral of St. George with Christian leaders: the Latin Patriarch of Jerusalem, His Beatitude Michel Sabbah; Bishop Kamal Bathish, Latin Patriarch of the Old City; and Bishop Riah Abu El-Assal, Anglican Bishop of Jerusalem. The three leaders spoke to World Methodist officers of their desire for peace and detailed their concerns about the decreasing presence of Christians in Israeli and Palestinian areas.

While the officers' agenda was dominated by organizational matters – it drafted a report on restructure to be presented at the 1999 Executive Committee meeting in Hong Kong – the continuing lack of peace in the land where Jesus lived, ministered, died and resurrected touched the officers deeply. They unanimously adopted a statement expressing solidarity with Palestinian Christians "who face pain and scars of injustice, hatred and oppression" in the land of their birth.[77]

"On an afternoon visit to Bethlehem, which is only six miles from Jerusalem, the Officers passed through the roadblock at Tantur where cars with Palestinian licenses plates are prevented from entering Jerusalem. Passing long lines of cars parked along both sides of the road, the Officers observed streams of workers on the Bethlehem side, walking up a long hill to the Israeli checkpoint where they presented identification cards to pass through for other transportation to get to their jobs in Jerusalem," reported the November-December 1998 issue of "World Parish."[78]

Peace was also at the heart of "Achieving the Vision," the $20 million endowment campaign approved in 1997 by the Executive Committee. Acknowledging the century-long support of World Methodism, a brochure nonetheless urges: "But so much remains undone; so many opportunities remain unfulfilled. Our brothers and sisters in faith from around the world – especially those of scarce means – look to the Council for resources to support crucial worldwide activities."[79]

The financial reality of Frances Alguire's term as chair of the World Methodist Council — indeed of every Council chair in recent memory -- was one of "hand to mouth," as Donald Fites, then chair of the finance committee, phrased it in his report to the Council in 2001. "The reality of our current situation is that we operate year in and year out with a deficit of $70,000 to $100,000. . . . It will take both sources of funding — funds from member churches and funds from the endowment -- for this Council to be enabled to translate the spirit and enthusiasm of these conferences into global reality for the over 75 million people who now live within Methodism's vast sphere of influence."[80]

The Millennium Tour

As the arrival of the year 2000 drew closer, Methodists around the world made plans to mark the closing of the second millennium since the birth of Jesus Christ and the beginning of the third millennium.

Among them was a ceremony in which candles, which had been lit in Bethlehem, were dispatched around the world to represent the spread of the light of Christ. As part of this ceremony, and in response to several invitations, Frances Alguire, with the support of WMC General Secretary Joe Hale and accompanied by her faithful husband, Donald, decided to visit countries in the Southern Hemisphere near the International Dateline – in effect, celebrating the turn of the millennium twice.

The tour was timed to conclude with a prestigious invitation that Dr. Alguire had already accepted: She was to represent World Methodism at Pope John Paul II's ecumenical millennium service in mid-January, 2000.

On Dec 28, 1999, Frances and Donald departed Chicago's O'Hare Airport in the evening to connect in Los Angeles with a 12½-hour flight to Auckland, New Zealand, followed by another nearly four-hour flight to the Pacific Island nation of Tonga. Crossing over the dateline, the Alguires arrived in Tonga at 10 p.m. on Dec. 30.

In Tongatapu they were met by Sina Vaipuna, secretary of the Methodist Church of Tonga, and Rev. Penisimani Fonua. Their welcome was a far cry from today's high-alert security measures: Sina took Frances for tea in a VIP lounge while Rev. Fonua helped Donald gather their luggage and clear customs. Once the baggage was in hand, their escorts drove the Alguires to Friendly Islander Hotel, about 35 minutes from the airport, where the owner – roused from sleep – led them to a two-bedroom cabin where incense burners were lit "to deter mosquitoes." Frances and Don located the light switches, closed the windows and turned on an electric fan before laying down for some much-welcomed rest.

On Dec. 31, Sina Vaipuna arrived at 9 a.m. to escort the Alguires to the Tonga Royal Palace for the presentation of New Year's gifts to His Majesty Taufa'ahau Tupou IV, and Her Majesty Halaevalu Mata'aho, the King and Queen of Tonga, who were both Methodists. The ceremony was graced by singing from the choir of Sia'atoutai Theological College.

Dignitaries waiting to present their gifts to the King and Queen sat on the grassy lawn in front of the palace, where Queen Halaevalu sat on a mat in the doorway. When a royal guide escorted Frances into the queen's presence, she followed Tongan etiquette and knelt in front of the queen to present her with a porcelain figure of an angel and a millennium date book.

An audience with the King

As the Alguires were about to leave, one of the ceremony guards instead steered them toward the palace for an audience with King Taufa'ahau. After a brief wait with Rev. Fonua on the palace verandah, Frances and Donald were ushered into the dining room and seated at a large table. All stood as the king entered, then Rev. Fonua sat on the floor at the opposite end of the table from the king, in accordance with Tongan custom.

Then Frances extended greetings to the king on behalf of World Methodists, and presented him with a gift: a star-shaped candle, which she proceeded to light with one of the Bethlehem candles after reading Matthew 5:14-15, "You are the light of the world…" After this sacred moment, she then gave the king another gift: a replica of the American Liberty Bell, a symbol of freedom. King Taufa'ahau, a historian himself, appeared pleased with the gift and started a conversation with the Alguires that lasted for 30 minutes. When ever-tactful Frances suggested that she and Don should leave, being aware that the king had a full schedule of New Year's activities, he insisted that first they share in some mango juice. "It was delicious," Frances recalled.

Sina Vaipuna was waiting patiently for their small group as they left the ceremonies. Together the foursome drove to the Methodist Church of Tonga and joined 4,000 "Camp 2000" participants for a sumptuous lunch. Then Frances and Donald joined in the event's sole English-language seminar, "The Bible and Culture," led by Dr. Puloka and Rev. Paulo Onoafe Latu.

Late in the afternoon, Sina drove Frances and Donald back to their tropical cottage for some rest before the evening's program of special thanksgiving services to mark the turn of the millennium. At 8 p.m. they joined the Royal Family, church leaders, ecumenical guests and 10,000 islanders in the beautiful city center park in Nuku'alofa for worship. The Rev. Dr. Alifaleti Mone, president of the Free Wesleyan Church of Tonga, presided at the multi-denominational service highlighted by the musical of multiple choirs. At midnight, as 1999 became 2000, the throng joined in singing "The Hallelujah Chorus" from Handel's "Messiah."

Worship at sunrise

Worship resumed at 5 a.m. on New Year's Day, when the Royal Family appeared again at the park to bring greetings during a praise service welcoming the dawning of the third millennium. That same day, a new administration center for The Methodist Church was opened by King Tupou IV. The large two-story building included offices of all the departments of the church and its president, general secretary, finance secretary and multiple meeting rooms.

Another high point of the Alguires' time in Tonga was a ceremony in which Frances presented the World Methodist Council's Order of Jerusalem, for outstanding service, to two longtime leaders: Rev. Dr. Sione A. Havea, and Her Royal Highness Princess Tuita, both of whom had served as members of the World Methodist Presidium.

Before Frances and Donald had left Tonga, Frances received a letter dated Jan. 3 from Queen Halaevalu Mata'aho, Chair of the Women's Department of the Tongan church, thanking Dr. Alguire in heartfelt terms for being with her nation as the New Year began.

Frances and Donald departed Tonga on Jan. 5 at the pre-dawn hour of 4 a.m. Despite their extremely early departure, Sina Vaipuna, Rev. Fonua and Dr. Puloka were at the airport to see them off with prayer and good wishes.

Aboard Polynesian Airlines, the Alguires flew about 90 minutes over the dateline to arrive in Apia, Western Samoa at 4:30 a.m. Tuesday, Jan. 4. Waiting for them at the Apia airport were two more longtime leaders of World Methodism: The Rev. Fa'atoese Auva'a, president of the Methodist Church of Western Samoa, and his devoted wife, Sunema Auva'a.

"Come see the president'

At the Hotel Insel Fehmarn in Apia, the Auva'as welcomed Donald and Frances with coffee and tea, and then informed them that an adjoining room was occupied by the Rev. H. Eddie Fox, director of World Methodist Evangelism, and his wife, Mary Nell. The Alguires and the Auva'as gently conspired to give the Foxes a surprising "wake-up call" by knocking on their door at 6 a.m. Dr. Fox, answering the door still in his pajamas, called out to his wife, "Mary Nell, come and see the president." There was a short time for the Alguires to tell the Foxes of their visit to Tonga before it was time for their hosts to escort Dr. and Mrs. Fox to the airport for their departure.

The Alguires were able to rest a few hours before attending the noon-time governor's reception and luncheon in honor of the 87th birthday of His Highness, the Head of State Susuga Malietoa Tanumafilia II, an event to which several hundred people had been invited. The event was hosted by Prime Minister Tuilaepa Sailele Malielegaoi and broadcast on local television. Dr. Alguire was escorted to the podium by the Samoan ambassador to New Zealand, so she could extend greetings from the World Methodist family to Western Samoa. Later the ambassador invited the Alguires for tea at her home, where her daughter, the Samoan Secretary of Education, joined them.

During their time in Western Samoa, Dr. Alguire met with Rev. Dr. Fineaso T.S. Faalafi, principal of the Methodist Piula Theological Seminary. Dr. Faalafi told his guest that the seminary had a great need for library publications, and for visits from guest lecturers, to improve the education of Methodist pastors in Western Samoa.

Frances also participated in a memorial service for Rev. Lene Milo, former president of Samoan Methodists. Conducted by Rev. Auva'a, the service included many denominational participants and mourners, all dressed in white according to Samoan funeral tradition. After the service, dinner was served by the family of the deceased to all who attended. Following another Samoan tradition, the family presented several gifts in his memory to government and church leaders and friends, as a tribute.

That evening Dr. Alguire spoke at a worship service led by Rev. Alfereti Samuelu. Later, she spoke to Samoan Methodist clergy during their time of spiritual renewal and shared in the dedication of a new Methodist Church building serving a rural area.

Next stop: New Zealand

On Jan. 8, the Alguires prepared for an 8 a.m. departure on Polynesian Airlines Flight 731 to New Zealand. When they arrived at the airport, however, there was no one present: No airline personnel, no officers, no access to telephones or even mailboxes.

While they waited at the airport, Sunema Auva'a was driven to a local pastor's home to telephone the airlines office. She was told that a large group had departed the previous evening, so that the next flight to Auckland had been rescheduled for noon that day. So the Alguires went back with the Auva'as to their home to have breakfast.

The delayed flight left the Alguires with a dilemma, however. The new arrival time in Auckland meant a tight connection to Christchurch, where Frances was scheduled to participate in a worship service that evening. They telephoned Rev. David Bush, president of the Methodist Church in New Zealand, to notify him of their problem, and he was "most understanding," Frances said.

When boarding time came, the Alguires discovered that the Auva'as had upgraded their economy class tickets to first class, to make up for the unexpected flight delay. As a result, even though they lost a day by re-crossing the International Dateline, Frances and Donald were able to get some rest during the 4½-hour flight, along with a four-course meal!

In Auckland, however, they were rushing to make their close connection to Christchurch when a sympathetic taxi driver came to their rescue. Giving up his number-two space in the waiting line, the driver agreed to take them on their short, fast trip. During their few minutes together in the taxi, the driver, Allan Wilkins, confided that he was searching for a church, and Frances and Donald invited him to consider becoming a Methodist. Then, as part of compensating him for the revenue he lost in accepting their short trip, they purchased an autographed copy of his just-released compact disc, "New Zealand 2000 The American Yacht Racing Song."

In Christchurch, which is known as "The Garden City," Frances and Don proceeded to Durham Street Methodist Church for a district worship service in the evening. After a brief historical summary of the church by Patricia Allan, Frances presented a message, "Strangers No More," in which she emphasized the unique kinship among the family of Christ. Among the worshippers were two World Methodist colleagues, Dr. Phyllis Guthart, former Presidium member, and Ruth Blundell, former Executive Committee member. After worship, participants joined in a meal and an informal session of questions and answers about the World Methodist Council.

Rev. Bush, the newly elected president, and former president Margaret Hamilton arranged a picnic for the next day, where the Alguires met with church leaders at the port city of Akaroa. The informal outing gave Frances time to meet and converse with more church leaders, including Judith and Basil Parks, Rev. Helen Buxton, the district superintendent; Peter and Nicola Grundy and Mr. and Mrs. Nevel Buxton.

On Jan. 11, 2000, the Alguires were escorted to the Papanui Church, where the Rev. Stan West was pastor, for "Tea and Conversation." Through questions about the participation of minority members in the World Methodist Council, Frances learned that the New Zealand church was struggling with its own sense of unity. Methodists of Maori descent in the Auckland area have an active congregation, but have little sense of conference-wide unity. Noting that the New Zealand conference's president and vice presidents serve for one year, Frances remarked that such a short term gives little time or insight to plan and implement long-range goals. Nonetheless, "I assured them that in the World Methodist Council, every voice had equal opportunity to be heard," Frances wrote in a remembrance. She encouraged the conference representatives to participate in World Methodist programs and share its work with their congregations.

At the conclusion, Frances was presented with a surprise: a commemorative special stamped envelope marking her official visit. Margaret Hamilton also presented her with a book, "Out of the Silence – Methodist Women of Aotearoa 1822-1985" by Ruth Fry, an Anglican author ("Aotearoa" is the Maori name for New Zealand).

On the afternoon of Jan. 11, the Alguires left Christchurch for Jakarta, Indonesia, by way of Singapore, having strengthened ties between the Methodist Church of New Zealand and the World Methodist Council.

Full circle in Indonesia

When the Alguires arrived at the Jakarta airport, a dear, longtime friend was waiting for them: Dr. Maimunah Natasha, a member of the World Methodist Council Executive Committee. Their Indonesia stop in many ways brought Frances full circle, for it was on a business trip with Donald years before that she had first learned how to enjoy the culture of a country as a solo visitor.

Maimunah – Indonesians typically use only one name – served as Frances' translator the next day when Frances addressed a group of Methodist clergy. After a worship service, Maimunah escorted Frances and Donald, along with Bishop Bachtiar Kwee and Jakarta District Superintendent Pat Jonatan to a visit with then-vice president Megawati Sukarnoputri. They were charmed by their visit, hardly suspecting that in a few short years Mrs. Sukarnoputri, daughter of longtime President Sukarno, would become Indonesia's president herself. They were surprised to come out of her office and find a huge group of television reporters all set up to interview this "famous lady" who received a personal interview with their Vice President.

After a lunch of Indonesian cuisine, the group went across Jakarta to a district gathering of Methodist women, where Dr. Alguire and Dr. Natasha were to speak. Their last evening in Indonesia included a service of prayer and worship at a young English-speaking Methodist congregation led by two American missionaries, Rev. Donald Turman and his wife Ramona Turner.

The Alguires' final morning in Jakarta was a somewhat somber affair. Meeting with leaders of the Communion of Churches in Indonesia,

Frances learned about the churches' ongoing efforts to foster dialogue regarding civil strife and political persecution of innocent residents. The knowledge she gained from her conversation with Indonesian church leaders led her to comment later, "We are called to remember members of our vast World family in daily prayers. Through our unity as faithful followers of Jesus Christ, we are called to give visible witness. We can make a difference in a troubled world."

On to Rome

From Jakarta, with a connection again in the island nation of Singapore off the tip of Malaysia, the Alguires headed for the last leg of the Millennium Tour: Rome.

Due in Rome for the Jan. 19 ceremony, Frances decided to spend an extra day in Frankfurt, Germany, to rest and recuperate from the time lag of crossing and re-crossing the International Dateline.

When the ecumenical service hosted by Pope John Paul II began, Dr. Alguire once again found herself both the only woman and the only layperson representing a worldwide communion. A photograph of the occasion shows her placed at the end of a row next to several Orthodox prelates with then-Archbishop of Canterbury, Dr. George Carey, at the opposite end. All of the clergy wore their traditional, often elaborate vestments, but Frances, true to her practice, wore her velvet suit and hat, along with the president's medallion of the World Methodist Council.

Upon the completion of her duties in Rome, Frances and Donald Alguire headed back to the United States. Although anticipating a two-hour drive from O'Hare Airport on Chicago's western edge to their home in New Buffalo, Michigan, they carried with them the satisfaction of beginning the third millennium since the birth of Jesus Christ with many new friendships and stronger ties for the World Methodist Council.

The Millennium Tour was one of the crowning events of Dr. Frances Alguire's term, which would end a little more than a year later. Her long-time colleague, His Eminence Sunday Mbang, retired Prelate of the Methodist Church of Nigeria, recalled the influence of Dr. Alguire's term in a remembrance:

"Frances was not just our leader, she was also the mother of the Officers of the World Methodist Council during the five years of her term. She was fond of bringing gifts to all the officers whenever and wherever we met. For the many years I have known Frances, she has never disappointed me in my belief in her. She is one of the few I know who loves everyone all the time equally. She neither discriminates against anybody nor looks down on anybody on the basis of tribe, class, region, color of the skin, name it.

"Many people in our world and some among the religious class practise 'chameleon' love. To date, some people, Christian and non-Christian, doubt the abilities of their colleagues because of where they come from. But Frances has always proven beyond all reasonable doubt that all people, irrespective of who they are and where they come from, were created equal by God. I had a personal experience of this discriminatory practice once upon a time. But Frances stood by me. The sad aspect of this incident was that this sad crime was perpetuated by a highly-placed religious leader. Many people suffered my fate but Frances had always come to their rescue. She had always stood by the victims, no matter the consequences.

"There is another aspect of Mrs. Alguire's life that is fascinating and very attractive. Frances by all standards is a successful American woman with a lot of experiences. But she is a very simple woman uncorrupted by the disease of the so-called 'civilized' people and people with affluence. She has remained a very simple and common Christian woman, always ready and willing to wine and dine with the unsophisticated, under-developed, common and down-trodden people rejected by others in the world. To this end, Frances has many friends all over the world and a lot of people who admire and respect her.

"Frances is not just a gift to the Methodist World alone, she was God's gift to our world."

The Millennium Tour

Even a heavy tropical rain couldn't keep Dr. Frances Alguire from attending the dedication of a new Methodist Church in a rural area of West Samoa. Standing to her left are Sunema and Fa'atese Auva'a, long-time leaders of the World Methodist Council and head of the Methodist Church of Samoa.

A gift of roasted pigs was one of the ways the Samoans welcomed their Methodist guests. With the help of Dr. Auva'a, Dr. Alguire was able to have her pig given to the hotel owner who provided housing for Frances and Donald during their visit.

In a rare photo of them together on their travels — since Don was usually behind the camera — Frances and Donald Alguire are shown as they leave their audience with the Queen of Tonga during the Millennium Tour in January 2000. The moment captures Frances in the performance of her duties as Chair of the World Methodist Council, and Don in his service as her companion and official photographer — their 50-plus years of mutual devotion and service to one another and Christ's Church.

In Tonga, Dr. Alguire preached at the largest Methodist Church there.

The Millennium Tour

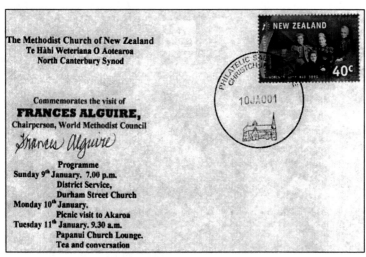

The Methodist Church of New Zealand
Te Hàhi Weteriana O Aotearoa
North Canterbury Synod

Commemorates the visit of
FRANCES ALGUIRE,
Chairperson, World Methodist Council

Programme
Sunday 9th January. 7.00 p.m.
District Service,
Durham Street Church
Monday 10th January.
Picnic visit to Akaroa
Tuesday 11th January. 9.30 a.m.
Papanui Church Lounge.
Tea and conversation

In New Zealand, the Methodist Church marked Dr. Alguire's visit with commemorative postage, including her schedule.

In Indonesia, Dr. Alguire met with then-Vice President Megawati Sukarnoputri, (later president July 2001 to October 20, 2004). With them are (from left) District Superintendent Pat Jonatan, WMC Executive Committee member Dr. Maimunah Natasha and Bishop Bachtlar Kwee.

The Millennium Tour

Dr. Frances Alguire's Millennium Tour for the World Methodist Council officially concluded with her participation in Pope John Paul II's ecumenical millennium service in January 2000. As can be seen in the photo, Dr. Alguire was the
only woman to represent a worldwide communion.   Vatican photo

Pope John Paul II
greets Dr. Alguire.
To the pope's right,
partially visible is
Cardinal Walter
Kasper, head of the
Vatican's ecumeni-
cal council.
Vatican photo

The Pursuit of Peace

Dr. Frances M. Alguire's term as Chair of the World Methodist Council was marked by a series of distinctive presentations of the World Methodist Peace Award to call attention to those seeking justice and human rights.

Frances Alguire presents the 1997 World Methodist Peace Award to Dr. Andrea Riccardi, representing the Catholic lay association, the Community of Sant'Egidio.

Estella Barnes de Carlotto, president of the Grandmothers of Plaza de Mayo, receives the 1999 World Methodist Peace Award from Frances Alguire and Rev. Joe Hale.

UN Secretary General Kofi Annan was honored in 1998 for his tireless efforts to negotiate peace worldwide.

United Nations photo

Nelson Mandela received the 2000 World Methodist Peace Award in Capetown, South Africa.

The Rev. Joe Hale received the 2001 Peace Award for 25 years as a global peacemaker.

Photos on this page, except for Dr. Kofi Annan, from United Methodist News Service

Highlights of Frances Alguire's Term

World Methodist Council officers posed for a photo after their installation at the 17th Conference in Rio de Janeiro, Brazil. In the first row (from left) are Bishop Prince A. Taylor (USA), Sunema Auva'a (Western Samoa), Kushnud Azariah (Pakistan), Bishop Sundo Kim (South Korea), Dr. Frances Alguire, His Eminence Sunday Mbang (Nigeria), Dr. Donald English (Great Britain) and assistant treasurer Edna Alsdurf (USA). In the second are (from left) are Bishop Neil Irons (USA), General Secretary Joe Hale, Geneva Secretary Ralph Young, Bishop Lawi Imathiu (Kenya), Dr. James Holsinger (USA), Dr. Maxie Dunnam (USA), Bishop Donald Ming (USA), Dr. John C.A. Barrett (Great Britain), Bishop Paulo Lockmann of Brazil and Dr. Olav Parnamets (Estonia).

Frances Alguire and Joe Hale in Rio de Janeiro.

Two months after her installation as Council Chair, Dr. Alguire spoke at the 1996 international panel at the Community of Sant'Egidio in Rome.

In 1997, Dr. Frances Alguire represented the World Methodist Council at the Lutheran World Federation's Ninth Assembly in Hong Kong.

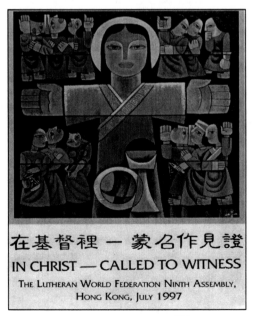

在基督裡 — 蒙召作見證

IN CHRIST — CALLED TO WITNESS

THE LUTHERAN WORLD FEDERATION NINTH ASSEMBLY, HONG KONG, JULY 1997

Christian artists in Hong Kong are noted for their vivid portrayals of Christ, as in this postcard from the Ninth Lutheran World Assembly.

Members of the World Methodist Council's Executive
Committee were thrilled to be seated on the portico of St.
Peter's Basilica during Pope John Paul II's weekly open-
air audience in September 1997. Despite his fragile health,
the pontiff came over to greet the officers personally.

Both attired in brilliant red,
Cardinal Walter Kasper and
Frances Alguire shared a
colorful moment at an
ecumenical gathering in
Barcelona, Spain.

Dr. Alguire joins a 1998 panel on women's
issues sponsored by Sant'Egidio. At left is
a Muslim panelist who told the assembly
that she could not be on a panel with
someone from the USA. Later she and
Mrs. Alguire became friends.

United Methodist-related Adrian College in Adrian, Michigan awarded Frances Alguire an honorary doctorate in June 1997, followed by Garrett-Evangelical Theological Seminary, which awarded her an honorary doctorate of humane letters that same month.

During their 1998 meeting, World Methodist Council officers visited the Methodist-founded Shepherd's Field nursery school in Beit Sahour, Israel.

Celebration in the Philippines

Dr. Alguire speaks at an assembly celebrating the 100th anniversary of the Methodist Church in the Philippines in 1998.

Dr. Alguire is surprised to find President Fidel V. Ramos of the Philippines standing in line to greet her.

Mrs. Grace Castro, wife of Bishop George Castro, created this presentation of a Psalm incorporating Dr. Alguire's name.

The creators of an appreciation certificate from Filipino Methodists apparently didn't know that Dr. Frances Alguire is a woman.

One Sunday while traveling through Georgia, the Alguires decided on a whim to visit the Baptist church in Plains, Georgia, where President Jimmy Carter was a member. Not only were President and Mrs. Roslyn Carter present that Sunday, he invited Frances to help teach his Sunday school class. President Carter received the World Methodist Peace Award in 1994.

While at a peace meeting in Bucharest, Romania, sponsored by the Community of Sant'Egidio in 1998, Frances and Donald met Sister Helen Prejean, a Catholic nun noted for her opposition to the death penalty. Frances would later join Sister Helen and other international religious leaders in signing a petition asking the United States to halt the death penalty.

One of Dr. Frances Alguire's more joyful journeys came in 2000 when she visited the Methodist Church of Korea. Here Dr. Alguire is welcomed with a gift from the Korean Methodist Women, with her friend and WMC colleague Mary Um seated behind at her left.

Also during her Korean visit, Dr. Alguire was seated with the leaders of the Korean Methodist Church during a time of prayer. Note the Korean tradition of wearing slippers, rather than typical outdoor shoes, inside the church.

In Spring 2001, shortly before the conclusion of her term as Chair of the World Methodist Council, Frances Alguire was an official observer at the World Council of Churches' Central Committee meeting. Seated to her left is World Methodist Council Geneva Secretary Ralph Young.

Often the Only Woman

As these photographs show, Dr. Frances Alguire was often the only women to represent a world Christian communion at global religious meetings during her 1996-2001 term

In 1997, Dr. Alguire represented World Methodist at a global interfaith meeting in Rome.

In 1998, Dr. Alguire was seated next to Dr. Konrad Raiser, general secretary of the World Council of Churches, at an interfaith meeting in Venice, Italy.

PREŞEDINŢIA ROM

Frances Alguire represented World Methodism at the 12th International Peace Conference sponsored by the Catholic lay association, the Community of Sant'Egidio in Bucharest, Rumania. While Dr. Claudio Bette speaks at the podium, Frances can be seen behind him to the left, responding to Dr. Denton Lotz, General Secretary of the Baptist World Alliance.

While in Bucharest, Frances was called upon to organize a memorial service for a United Methodist teenager who was killed in a car wreck. The service was led by Orthodox and Catholic priests with Frances reading a prayer she wrote.

Frances with Monsignor Paglia of the Community of Sant'Egidio and Orthodox Patriarch Teoctist of Rumania in Bucharest.

161

Chapter 5

To Brighton and Beyond

On the evening of July 26, 2001, Dr. Frances M. Alguire, attired in a gleaming white summer suit, stepped up to the microphone in the cavernous main hall of the Brighton Center in the British seaside resort of Brighton. Her day had been one of the longest and most challenging of her life. From early morning, the first day of the 18th World Methodist Conference had been so packed with events requiring her presence that there had barely been time to spend a few minutes apart with God, let alone eat and rest.

Now was the culminating moment of her historic term as the first lay woman to chair the World Methodist Council. She stood before an audience of some 3,000 delegates to deliver the message at the grand opening worship ceremonies of the first World Methodist Conference of the 21st century. Her petite frame was dwarfed even more by the enormous red, blue and gold banners behind her, brilliantly proclaiming the conference's theme: "Jesus Christ, God's Way of Salvation." As the room quieted, Dr. Alguire began to speak:

I told you this morning what a wonderful group of leaders and Presidium members the Council had elected five years ago. Our five years together have gone quickly and as we prayed and prepared for the program of this week, we were praying about our opening worship service this evening. I discerned that this message should be given by some renowned Evangelical speaker, but several of our brothers discerned it should be me as Chairperson of the Council. So I stand before you, the first lay woman to chair the Council, and a lay woman to give the first message of our worship together in the 21st century.

After a moment of prayer, inviting the presence of God's Holy Spirit, Dr. Alguire continued:

We are here, not as a body of worshippers on a life-long quest for truth and holiness, nor as intellectuals driven by academic curiosity, or as persons driven by a penchant for controver-

163

sy and debate; but rather, we come as witnesses, chosen by God to serve, to know, and to believe in Jesus Christ, God's way of salvation. This 18th World Methodist Conference, the first to meet in the 21st century, is unique. We are here from over 100 countries, representing 74 denominations, all with Wesleyan roots and united as followers of Jesus Christ. A question for each of is, what does our Conference theme, "Jesus Christ, God's Way of Salvation," mean for us as witnesses and servants in our world parish today. Are we serving the church of Jesus Christ in the most caring and servant-like way? A world of boisterous noises, interruption, warfare, injuries and illness, plus unexpected demands and daily routines, which often keep us from a time of quiet reflection, time of meditation and prayer; and a time to hear the soft, gentle voice of an ever-present God to discern what new thing God would have us be about; I have never heard some say at the end of the day, "I have read the Bible too much, I have thought of others too much or I have prayed too much." Being a Christian in the 21st century is different from that of our grand-parents' time — teaching truth and morality and the world of scripture is still very important. But in today's world it must be communicated with diverse cultural, ethnic and social groups.

We now live on a planet with instant means of global com-munication. The Internet is of great benefit to keep us informed, but like other means of communication, it is often used to project programs and images which are not beneficial to humanity. With all the changes in the world, God's spirit and scripture are never changing. John Wesley thought for ways to express spiritual life throughout the day. He found a way in what he called "the means of grace." His message was through spiritu-al discipline, which people used to express their faith, and in a time of sharing and quietness received God's grace. As witnesses we are called to develop a perspective and skills necessary to relate the gospel message to the foes yet waiting to hear the word of Christ. Since the genesis of Wesleyan Methodism, we know the importance of evangelism and social action.

Dr. George Morris reminds us that word and deed are as

important as breathing in and breathing out. Whichever one is more important depends upon which you did last. Our reason for being and doing is grounded in scripture. We come to know more about Jesus Christ through daily prayer, scripture reading and a time of quiet reflection for discernment as we try to perceive the new thing God would have us be about.

I'm reminded of a preacher who was writing a sermon. His small son came into the room and asked him, "How do you know what to write or to say?" The preacher said, "I listen to God." "The young son said, "Then why do you keep erasing?"

How often do we ignore the still, small voice and then proceed to do our own thing? Gathering as a world family causes each of us to open our eyes and minds to the fact that we can no longer live in our own small world. We are each called and created to make a difference, to provide leadership and direction in new ways, and to each do our part as believers, united in Christ, to remove and eliminate barriers of racism, sexism, ageism, elitism and the other "isms" that separate us, God's people. We can help overcome hatred, distrust and apathy by sharing the love of Christ with all people and by developing the one important "ism," spiritualism.

Henri J. Nouwen writes that theological reflection is reflecting on the painful and joyful realities of every day with the mind of Jesus, and thereby raising human consciousness to the knowledge of God's gentle guidance. Christian leaders cannot simply be persons who have well-informed opinions about the burning issues of our time. Their leadership must be rooted in the permanent, intimate relationship with the incarnate Word, Jesus. It is there that we find the source for our words, advice and guidance. Through contemplative prayer we need to listen again and again to the voice of love, to find the courage and wisdom to address whatever issue presents itself. It is then that we can respond anew to the words which Jesus read in the synagogue from the prophet Isaiah, and now as recorded in Luke 4:18-18:

"The spirit of the Lord is upon me because he anointed me to bring good news to the poor. He has sent me to proclaim release to the captives, and recovery of sight to the blind, to let the oppressed go free and to proclaim the year of the Lord's favor."

Finnish composer Sibelius, in an interview concerning the methods of composition, said he strove that through music there must run a golden chord of truth. This golden chord of truth should be the linkage for all that we are about. A message, however lofty, must be personally believed and experienced if it is to avail. When you see the word God, with the big, round "O" in the center, this is the link that should be extended to reach out to all of God's creation. This mystical union can be experienced in a variety of ways, such as through intimate friendship and being an enabler to others, by reaching out in a spirit of love and caring as Christians. We heard in 2 Corinthians: "So if anyone is in Christ, there is a new creation." Can you imagine being made new from the inside out, from the very roots of our being? The old has passed away. The new has come and our lives are transformed from self-centered, self-seeking agendas to a Christ-centered life in which our thoughts and ambitions are no longer focused on ourselves but on Christ and the interests of others. Love, duty and service become new priorities. There is a transformation of values when we encounter disappointments, hardships and suffering. Instead of being tragedies, those unexpected events become the means of God's grace and challenge to help us grow strong in faith.

Recently my doctor sent me to a hematologist because I had been having low hemoglobin for a period of time. This hematologist, who is a well-know specialist in my area, Dr. Muthasamy, is a Muslim. The day I went for my appointment, he looked at me and first he asked how old I was. Well, he had that in my record, but then he said, "What do you do?" As he was a physician, I told him, "A registered nurse, now retired." [But again] he asked, "What do you do?" I think my doctor must have told him because I told my regular doctor that he had to keep me in shape for five years. So I could see that Dr. Muthasamy was probing for more, so I said, "I am currently Chairperson of the World Methodist Council." He said, "I have been reading the Koran and [Mohammed] said God is the God of love, [so] how can he let a child die of cancer?" I said to him, "We do not know God's answers, but we are called to share in love and caring with all humanity." Since then we have had many more conversations and have become great friends.

The transformation of accepting Christ fully into our lives gives us new understanding of people we meet each day, plus an appreciation for the beauty of God's creation and our love for the human family. All our experiences can be seen in a new light; to see God in everything makes life a great adventure. All this is from God who reconciled us to himself through Christ and has given us the ministry of reconciliation without counting our sins against us . . . that familiar verse from 2 Corinthians. Christ draws close to us. Sometimes his presence is not made known by flaming light or angelic song but by the gradual recognition of something we experience daily enmeshed in our lives like salt or leaven. When we say yes to becoming a follower of Jesus Christ our lives take on new meaning.

It was at age eight that I responded to an altar call at a Methodist camp meeting. Someone asked me recently if as a child I ever thought I would be the first woman to chair the World Methodist Council, I quickly said "no, and not even as an adult." I can attest to the fact that when you say yes to becoming a follower of Jesus Christ, your life takes on new meaning in a glorious and unimaginable way. Our greatest mission as world Methodists today is to tell the world about the love of God and to show that we are believers, not only through our word, but through our action.

This evening we come to commune together and to partake of the broken bread and wine in remembrance of Christ's sacrifice, for the forgiveness of sin and the promise of eternal life. The gospels remind us of the institution of the Lord's supper in those verses read by Dr. Karen Westerfield Tucker. "While they were eating, Jesus took a loaf of bread and after blessing it, gave it to the disciples and said, "Take, eat, this is my body." Then he took the cup and after giving thanks he gave it to them saying,

"Drink from it, all of you, for this is my blood of the covenant which is poured out for many for the forgiveness of sin." As we prepare to receive the sacrament freely given to all who are believers of Christ, or those who are desiring to know Christ in a deeper way, we come with a sense of forgiveness for all that is past and the opportunity of a new beginning. This is a time to rekindle the flame within us that our hearts, like Wesley's, may be strangely warmed. John Wesley reminded early followers with these words: "Nor yet do thou say I must do something before I come to Christ. Expect Christ even now. He is nigh."

The Christian life involves more than growth and development. It involves transformation of ourselves anew for God who created us and sustains us. Christian faith is about an inner transformation resulting from an encounter with the living Christ. We make hundreds of decisions each day . . . who knows how many in a lifetime . . . yet only one [decision] is of supreme, eternal importance. That one decision is to follow Christ in all that stands between here and eternity. When anyone is united in Christ, there is a new creation. The old order has gone and a new order has begun. As followers of Jesus Christ, we are called to perceive what new thing God would have us be about, and then without hesitation, do it. Would the congregation join me in saying — Amen.[1]

Five years' work

Frances Alguire's message to the 18th World Methodist Conference encapsulated the deepest desire of her heart over the course of her five-year term as Chair of the World Methodist Council: That Methodists around the globe, transformed through intimate relationship with Jesus Christ, would spread the knowledge of God's love everywhere through witnessing to their faith in words and deeds. In other words, every action, every appearance, every statement she made between 1996 and 2001 in her official capacity was rooted in a broad understanding of the task of evangelism — "telling the good news of Jesus Christ."

This goal also laid the foundation for the 18th World Methodist Conference at which she presided.

The Rev. H. Eddie Fox, longtime World Director of Evangelism for the Council, attested to Dr. Alguire's capacity as a an evangelist: "Dr. Alguire never thought of herself as a pioneer but a servant leader. She never tired of encouraging children, political and church leaders, including the Pope. Always she was the evangelist, the bearer of good news whether in the islands of the Pacific or the teeming cities in the world. She was never ill at ease inviting persons to prayer and Christian ministry. I have witnessed her inviting persons to prayer in many different circumstances. She is one of the most powerful ambassadors of the World Methodist Movement and a faithful witness of the gospel. Because of Fran Alguire we have footprints that are always pointing the way of Jesus. She always radiates joy!"[2]

The Rev. Hal Brady, whom Frances and Donald Alguire had shepherded through the 1991 conference in Singapore, identified a spiritual virtue in Frances that drew him into greater participation in the Council's work: God's grace, which manifested itself through her personal graciousness to others.

"When Fran became the first woman president of the Council, I was asked to chair the Program Committee for the 2001 World Methodist Conference that was held in Brighton, England," Dr. Brady said in a remembrance. "With that enlarging responsibility, I had opportunity to work closely with Fran for the next five years as we prepared for that Conference. I found Fran to be a great leader with a heart for inclusiveness. She always put others and their needs first. Her ability to listen was/is phenomenal.

"In addition, Fran was a wise leader ever making decisions that were in the best interest of World Methodism and the Council itself. As President, she was a worldwide ambassador for Christ and the Council and traveled extensively in carrying out her duties. She was totally comfortable traveling to the most glamorous cities or the most backward areas of the world. She met the well-known and the lesser known figures of the world exactly the same. Always, Fran's beautiful smile and caring spirit would win the day.

"Being part of the World Methodist Council has enriched my life in a very significant way. It has definitely defined my ministry, enlarged my vision and broadened my horizons. Fran Alguire was the one who made it possible, and I will be forever grateful."[3]

Inspired by Dr. Alguire's example, Dr. Brady and the international Conference Program Committee set up a schedule of presentations, workshops, seminars and performances designed to proclaim the historic faith in Jesus Christ as it challenged participants to set their witness to the faith in 21st century contexts.

A bigger picture of Jesus

The conference opened the morning of July 21, 2001 with a keynote address that defined the new context in which Methodists lived and worked. Dr. David Wilkinson, British astrophysicist and pastor, presented a video titled "Power of Ten," in which he described the reality of the Creator from the inner workings of the tiniest subatomic particle to the vast outer reaches of the universe. The conference was silent in amazement as the video went from a picture of a family having a picnic in a park to a view of planet and galaxies, and then in an opposite direction down to the inside of a cell nucleus, with the spiral coils of DNA. And Dr. Wilkinson translated for the crowd the immensity of what they had just seen.

"My friends, do we need to get a bigger picture of God? I'm a male Christian. At times in the past and still today man through power structures and oppression have limited the opportunities for creation. But Jesus, lord of creation, is bigger than that. I'm a white Anglo-Saxon. I value my history and my heritage, but at times in the past and still today, whites have limited opportunity and justice for those of different ethnic origins. But Jesus, the spiraler of DNA, is bigger than that. I'm a British Methodist. I value that, but sometimes it seems to me that we British Methodists, because it all started here, sometimes think that we are the center of the kingdom of God. A friend of mine from another culture just taught me a little bit, he said, "You British, you doubt everything in theology apart from your God-given right to tell the rest of us what to believe." But Jesus, the Lord of a hundred billion galaxies, is bigger than us. I'm an Evangelical Christian. I rejoice in the authority of scripture, the centrality of the cross, the importance of evangelism, but I have to say I often look down upon other Christians of different traditions. But Jesus the Lord of creation is bigger than that.

" . . . So my friends, is Jesus big enough in your vision today? Big enough to communicate not only in your culture, but in another culture? Big enough to relate to both men and women — black and white — elderly and young. Is Jesus big enough to be both Lord of personal religious experience and Lord of science — my local church and the worldwide church?

"How do you get a bigger picture of God's salvation, my friends? You see his way of salvation includes reaching individuals who have not heard the name of Jesus, or as often is the case in Western culture, who reject him or see no relevance in him. This means that vibrant evangelism and imaginative apologetics are not an option for the few, it's an imperative for church, for God wants to reconcile all people to himself. Step back, and get a bigger picture."[4]

'Big picture' lenses

From Dr. Wilkinson's electrifying keynote address, participants at the 18th World Methodist Conference spread out to don several "lenses" to gain a bigger picture of Jesus Christ for the 21st century. Even John Wesley could not have envisioned a world parish as large and complex as the global context that faced participants at the 2001 conference.

The program included 16 major seminars on such topics as "Spirituality in the 21st Century," "Common Faith, Common Witness: The Mutual Challenge to Ecumenism and Evangelism," "Christian Faith and Education in the 21st Century," and "Faith Under Fire: Issues and Challenges of the Dawning Millennium." Likewise there were 16 practical workshops such as "Effective Use of Small-Group Ministries," "Teaching the Bible for All Ages," "Reclaiming the Ministry of Healing," "A Christian Response to Economic Injustice," "Multi-Cultural Ministries," "AIDS Care — Caring for AIDS Caregivers" and "Partners with a Purpose: The Role of Lay Persons in Disciple-Making."

Leadership at the 18th World Methodist Conference also reflected the inclusive model of its Chair, Frances Alguire. Many of the most respected theologians and scholars of World Methodism led workshops and seminars alongside lay leaders and young people of many nations. In addition, the role of women was heightened at the Brighton conference, with one of the day's keynote addresses, "Sharing the Way," presented by Dr. Mariela Michailova of Bulgaria, and three days of Bible study led by the Rev. Grace Imathiu, a Kenyan Methodist serving in Green Bay, Wisconsin.

As various leaders shared freely of their witness and skills with conference participants, Dr. Alguire continued in both her ceremonial and administrative functions.

Before the conference started, she was the guest speaker at a reception for World Methodist leaders held by the Mayor of Brighton. She opened a new exhibit of Christian art at Brighton University, and gave the message at the dedication of a new Methodist Church in the city. Local television and radio stations interviewed her about the conference.

Amid all her formal duties, Frances was still making new friends. Among them was Professor Gustavo Jacques Diaz Alvim of Brazil, making his first trip to a World Methodist Conference.

"From the first day of the Conference I could feel her leadership, her consecration and devotion to Christ, her love for the Methodist Church and her dedication to the tasks of chairperson," Dr. Alvim wrote in a remembrance.[5] "Like a permanent dynamo she was always present in all activities, giving important contributions.

"In Brighton something unexpected happened in my life. Something that I didn't expect, neither imagined: I was elected one of the Presidium officers of the World Methodist Council. Since then I have had the great privilege to know many Methodist leaders and I have especially had other opportunities to talk to my friend Dr. Alguire in meetings that took place during the five years while she was honorary president (2001-2006) of WMC. She has always been active and hopeful. Her words are opportune about different subjects, plans and problems, but I'm impressed by her care for people, her attention to everyone, and working for Methodist Church. Her steadfast faith, her zealous prayers, her resolute testimony, her agreeable friendship were precious examples for my life."

Two days before the conference began its rounds of seminars, workshops, worship services and drama and music performances, Dr. Alguire prepared to preside at the meeting of the 500-member World Methodist Council. The work of five years was coming to fruition in an agenda that included:

- Formal ratification by the Council of the $20-million 'Achieving the Vision Endowment Campaign,"
- A resolution from the Social and International Affairs Committee advocating the Jubilee campaign to forgive international debt;
- Reports from the standing committees on Ecumenics and Dialogue; Education, Evangelism, Family Life, Theological Education, Worship and Youth;
- Exploration of a World Methodist Council relationship with The Salvation Army, which has roots in Methodism through its founder, William Booth;
- A constitutional change that would ensure that the president of the World Methodist Youth would be a part of the Presidium, along with continued discussion of the Council's purpose and structure, especially how to assure broad, diverse representation from member churches;
- Reports from the youth federation and the World Federation of Methodist and Uniting Church Women, and the World Federation of Methodist and Uniting Church Men.[6]

As Council members prepared to act on these and other events, they could not exclude the impact of happenings in the world outside the conference. For instance, dozens of delegates had been unable to attend because they could not obtain British visas, a problem that had occurred consistently at every Conference. Council member Don Kirkland moved that the Council send a letter to British Prime Minister Tony Blair about the issue. Dr. Richard Heitzenreiter reminded the Council that each country has its own visa regulations, and the British Host Committee offered its own frustration at the visa situation. Mr. Kirkland withdrew his motion after the president and vice president of the British Methodist Conference offered to send a letter about the situation on the Council's behalf.

One of the ironies of the visa conflict, however, was that among those denied visas to attend the conference was a past Chairman, Bishop Lawi Imathiu. Because he was unable to obtain a visa to Great Britain, he missed seeing his daughter, the Rev. Grace Imathiu, inspire the conference as one of the first African clergywomen to present the Bible study. Sadly, Bishop Imathiu also missed his first opportunity to meet his new grandson, Erik Mugambi, the son of Rev. Imathiu and her husband, the noted nature artist and photographer David Hay Jones. Rev. Imathiu used the episode in her Friday morning Bible study as an example of how the rules of governments around the world can keep families apart, that people from some countries — such as her son, an American by birth — are automatically more privileged than others such as her father, who had given his life to Christ's Church and the World Methodist Council.[7]

The troubles of the world intruded as well. Dr. Ajith Fernando of Sri Lanka was unable to travel to Brighton to lead Bible study as planned because his island country's airport had been bombed by terrorists. And everyone attending got a taste of how climate change was affecting Europe, as unseasonably high summer temperatures, well into the 90s by Fahrenheit scale, broiled all of southern England. The extreme heat had one benefit, however. It helped ensure good attendance at the seminars and workshops held in the air-conditioned confines of the Brighton Center, even if it meant that delegates sometimes caught up on sleep they didn't get the night before while staying in hot, un-air-conditioned hotel rooms.

Passing on leadership

The 18th World Methodist Conference in Brighton was also notable for the retirement of the Rev. Joe Hale after 25 years as General Secretary of the World Methodist Council and the installation of the Rev. George H. Freeman as the first General Secretary of the new millennium.

Dr. Freeman recalled his first encounter with Dr. Alguire.

"I first met Fran Alguire at the 2000 General Conference of the United Methodist Church in Cleveland, Ohio," he wrote in a remembrance.[8] "She impressed me as a highly energetic woman who was extremely knowledgeable about the Church and its inner workings.

"At that time I was in the process of applying for the position of General Secretary of the World Methodist Council, and she was the Chairperson of the Council. I began to know Fran Alguire at a deeper level beginning with my interview for the position I now hold.

"I learned of her insightfulness and of her desire to match individuals skills, experiences and talents with the task that is to be performed. This insight manifested itself in every appointment, nomination and assignment which the World Methodist Council gives to various individuals in order to accomplish a task. She helped see that this was accomplished as the Council was best able to do so.

"Following my interview, my name was advanced to the Nominating Committee of the Council, and ultimately to the full Council meeting in 2001 in Brighton, England, when I was elected General Secretary. Throughout the entire process beginning with the application process for the position of General Secretary, to the election in Brighton, she was most helpful to my wife, Virginia, and me, helping us to grasp the global nature of World Methodism and her experience and connections within this family."

Dr. Freeman said that what impressed him most about Frances Alguire was the esteem with which she is held by Methodists around the world. "I quickly learned that she is highly respected around the world, and that Methodist/Wesleyan people have deep admiration for her friendship and for her leadership abilities. She is a caring person who takes time to listen and who exhibits great compassion and concern for the concerns and needs of people and Churches.

"Fran is always eager when learning of a need in a particular Church around the world to try and match that Church with person or persons who have the skills and ability to offer help. She exhibits the Methodist 'connection' greatly in this way!"[9]

Beyond Brighton

Dr. Frances Alguire's service didn't end when she passed her president's badge to His Eminence Sunday Mbang, the 2001-2006 Chair of the World Methodist Council. As honorary president, she continued to serve on the Council's Presidium, and to respond as she could to invitations to speak, write and teach.

Rev. George Freeman noted that one of Dr. Alguire's major contributions since her term ended has been her ongoing support of the World Methodist Council's Evangelism program.

"Fran's passion for the Church's ministry of making disciples for Jesus Christ continues to this day," Dr. Freeman wrote in a remembrance. "Her support of the Division of World Methodist Evangelism, her prayer support for the Council's leadership, and her reliable presence at meetings of the Council, Executive Committee, Officers and task forces to which she may be asked to serve are testimonies to the 'Methodist DNA' that is in her!"[10]

Mary Um, General Secretary of the Board of Social Responsibility & Laity of the Korean Methodist Church and a member of Honorary Order of Jerusalem, wrote in a remembrance that she continues to find her longtime friend to be a spiritual leader of World Methodism.

"I have worked with the WMC since 1986 when I attended the 15th World Methodist Conference in Nairobi, Kenya," Ms. Um wrote.[11] "I first met Dr. Frances Alguire in September 1987 where we were both members of an Executive Committee meeting Ocho Rios, Jamaica.

"In that meeting we did a heavy discussion concerning the next WMC meeting, whether it should accept the invitation to be held in Singapore or Korea. In the end we from Korea lost the bid for the 16th WMC Conference. I will never forget the vivid memory of the meeting and the impression I had of Dr. Alguire. I confess I saw her as a very typical American lady who was determined with a strong mind.

"At the 16th WMC meeting in Singapore in July 1991 we were both elected officers and became members of the Presidium. Gradually I got to know her better and saw her leadership abilities and self-confidence. I felt that Dr. Alguire was such a lovely Methodist lady and the quality of her friendship was very gorgeous. She has a talented mind and is always cooperative.

"During her five-year tenure as WMC chairperson she visited Seoul Korea on several occasions. She shared very precious time with the people of Korea. She used to preach in local churches on Sunday mornings and addressed various meetings, I thought she was one of the outstanding preachers as she was such a good communicator of Wesleyan theology."[12]

Ms. Um said she found that one of Dr. Alguire's greatest gifts was her ability "to bring together people of various cultures, races and backgrounds to come to one mind."

"During the time preparations were underway for the 19th World Methodist Conference to be held in Seoul, Korea, there broke out a terrible opposition," Ms. Um continued. "Some Korean leaders became very critical of the Korean leaders where the meeting was to be held. They were dwelling on past mistakes that went back 30 years. Frances Alguire asked me confidentially if the allegations were true. We both agreed that you can not dwell on mistakes done 30 years ago, and we believed they were forgiven and that we needed to move forward. I admired her understanding and leadership."

Ms. Um also said that Dr. Alguire helped her during a difficult time at the 2004 United Methodist General Conference in Pittsburgh, Pennsylvania.

"I was a delegate from Korea to the United Methodist General Conference. In that meeting the North American session leaders invited the World Methodist leaders from other parts of the world that were attending the conference to talk about the next 19th WMC meeting to be held in Seoul, Korea," Ms. Um wrote in a remembrance.[13]

"I was given an opportunity to speak, to invite them to Korea. I had written my speech in English and memorized it, as English is very difficult for me. Many Bishops and other dignitaries came to listen to me. Seeing those many people made me forget the speech I had memorized. I could only keep saying 'Let us come to Korea all together and bring your friends.' I continued saying the same thing, but I was so embarrassed and became so shy, my face turned red. But in that situation Dr. Alguire came to my rescue and comforted me and encouraged me, so I could speak."

A new home

As Frances and Donald Alguire approached their 80s, they became aware that it was time to enter a new era in their life. With daughter Mary Papish in Chicago, and daughter Catherine Alguire in Chapel Hill North Carolina, they decided it would be best to move closer to some family. Plus after nearly eight decades of Midwest winters, they relished the thought of a more temperate climate.

So in 2002, they sold the dream home they'd built in New Buffalo, Michigan, in 1990, and moved into a smaller home in Chapel Hill, North Carolina, near their daughter Catherine, now an Occupational Therapist and a specialist in landscape design. One of their first actions upon moving was to join a United Methodist congregation. They moved their membership to Chapel Hill University United Methodist Church, coming symbolically full circle from the Chapel Hill Methodist Church they'd helped to found in Michigan in the mid-1950s. Then in 2006 they moved into a two-bedroom condominium in the Cedars Retirement Community in Chapel Hill.

Yet while Frances and Donald relieved themselves of the management of a large home and the possessions of their younger years, they remain active. They volunteer as host and hostess for their retirement center, welcoming visitors with the same hospitality they've always shown. They exercise daily and continue to travel. In July 2007 they attended a major event for World Methodist Evangelism at Simpsonwood Conference Center in north Georgia, then embarked on a 10-day cruise and tour of Alaska,. Unfortunately, because of Donald Alguire's sudden illness, they were forced to cancel their planned trip to Sydney, Australia, for a World Methodist Council Executive Committee meeting. "It was the first Council meeting we've missed in 30 years," Frances lamented.

Elder wisdom

In its Winter 2003 issue, the alumni magazine of Adrian College in Michigan published an interview with Dr. Frances Alguire (FA in the excerpt below) written by Darcy Gifford (DG in the excerpt). Among her responses, Frances summed up her faith for a new generation:

DG: We live in a time when terror threats are abundant and images of violence are depicted regularly on the nightly news. What strategies do you suggest for keeping faith in these turbulent times?

FA: Tennyson wrote years ago, "More things are wrought by prayer than this world dreams of." The World Methodist Community totals over 75 million members throughout the world. Many members of this family are praying daily for peace for all of the world, and others are actively engaged in marches for peace and letter writing campaigns to leaders of countries that think war is the only solution.

We keep the faith by remembering that God's love, grace and abiding presence are always here — we are the ones that stray. Also, as we meet with others in the community of faith, support is generated. Our words have power — power to encourage or to discourage.

Let me share a verse from the Revised English Bible, Jude 1:20: "But you, my friends, must make your most sacred faith the foundation of your lives. Continue to pray in the power of the Holy Spirit."[14]

Dr. Monica Attias, a leader of the Catholic lay association, the Community of Sant'Egidio, said in a remembrance that Dr. Alguire's ongoing participation in her organization's activities showed that age is no impediment to Christian service.

Frances Alguire with Francesca Scampi and Dr. Monica Attias of Sant'Egidio Community.

"When she retired, she still continued to take part in the Interfaith Prayer for Peace," Dr. Attias wrote. "In 2003, in Germany, she agreed to give a speech on the theme "The Elderly: The Wisdom of Peace." She said something very touching and true, as a person who does not fear her age but rather carries the responsibility of what she has seen and lived through:

"Those of us who are 76 or older have lived through a number of global conflicts, civil strife and warfare. We have witnessed the loss of human life in addition to mass destruction of homes and infrastructure . . . The elderly have learned that the welfare of humanity is more important than selfish material gains."

"This is, I think, a great contribution towards peace," Dr. Attias concluded.[15]

From a country girl in a one-room school in Michigan, to registered nurse, to busy young wife and mother, to innovative church leader, to global traveler and activist, to the first laywoman to lead World Methodism — the gifts of Frances Maxine Werner Alguire have been one great, lifelong contribution toward faith and peace.

The Road to Brighton

Officials of the World Methodist Council and others planning the 2001 World Methodist Conference stand in front of the Royal Pavilion in Brighton, England. They are (from left): DeWayne Woodring, conference coordinator; Edith Ming, secretary of the Council's Program Committee; Frances M. Alguire, chairperson of the Council's Executive Committee; Val Kampf of Sovereign Tourism in London; the Rev. Hal Brady, chairman of the 2001 Program Committee; and Bill Haire, president of Travelink in Nashville, Tenn.

United Methodist News Service Photo

Dr. Alguire initials an agreement with John Brightman, general manager of the Brighton Centre (also seated) for the 2001 World Methodist Conference. Looking on is John C.A. Barrrett, a member of the Council.

United Methodist News Service Photo

Passing on Leadership

Dr. Frances Alguire (front right) concluded her term by presiding over the 18th World Methodist Conference in Brighton, England, with the theme "Jesus Christ: God's Way of Salvation." At the conclusion of the conference, a new slate of World Methodist leaders took office: (from left) His Eminence Sunday Mbang, prelate of the Methodist Church of Nigeria and Dr. Alguire's successor as Council President; Dr. John C.A. Barrett, 2001-2006 Vice Chair; Dr. Gustavo Jacques Diaz Alvim; Bishop Clarence Carr of the African Methodist Episcopal Church, Zion; Bishop Walter Klaiber of The United Methodist Church in Germany; Maimunah Natasha of Indonesia; Bishop Neil Irons of The United Methodist Church in the United States; Dr. Earle L. Wilson, The Wesleyan Church; Laurie Day of World Methodist Youth; Dr. Denis C. Dutton of the Methodist Church of Malaysia, incoming Geneva Secretary; Rev. George Freeman, incoming General Secretary; Rosemary Wass, President of the World Federation of Methodist and Uniting Church Women; Dr. James Holsinger, Council Treasurer; and Rev. Joe Hale, outgoing General Secretary.

Frances Alguire renewed acquaintances with colleagues Mary Um of Seoul, South Korea (right); Bishop Paulo Lockmann of Brazil (center) and Dr. Winston Worrell of the World Methodist Evangelism Institute (left of Dr. Alguire) during the 2004 United Methodist General Conference in Pittsburgh, Pennsylvania.

Serving as honorary president through the 2001-2006 term gave Dr. Alguire opportunity to keep in touch with friends such as Katherine Ng of Hong Kong when they attended an officers' meeting in Abuja, Nigeria.

World Methodist Conference in Seoul, South Korea

At the 19th World Methodist Conference in Seoul, South Korea, in 2006, Frances had the opportunity to get reacquainted with some of the ladies from Kum Nan Methodist Church, which she had helped to dedicate while WMC Chair.

Still serving the World Methodist Council with their wisdom and experience during its meeting in Seoul are past presidents Bishop Lawi Imathiu of Kenya and Dr. Frances Alguire, shown here with Bishop William Hutchinson of The United Methodist Church.

Leaders of the World Methodist Council led a worship for Peace and Unification in Korea at the border between North Korea and South Korea during the 19th World Methodist Conference based in Seoul, South Korea, in July 2006. From left are: Mary Um, Korean Methodist Women; a Korean representative; Dr. Eddie Fox, World Methodism Evangelism; Bishop Clarence Carr; Dr. Frances Alguire; Bishop Kyoung Ha Shin, president of the Korean Council of Bishops; His Eminence Sunday Mbang, 2001-2006 Chair of the World Methodist Council; Dr. John C.A. Barrett, 2006-2011 Chair of the Council; Dr. George Freeman, General Secretary; Dr. James Holsinger, Council treasurer.

Participants at the 2006 World Methodist Conference released hundreds of balloons containing prayers for peace and reunification of Korea while at the border between North Korea and South Korea.

'A Firm Faith and a Warm Heart'

A Special Remembrance by the Rev. Dr. John C.A. Barrett
2006-2011 President of the World Methodist Council

A few years ago I met P.D. James, the British writer responsible for some of the best recent crime novels. I had invited her to be the guest of honor at my college Speech Day. Her appearance was not what I expected from the creator of Commander Adam Dalgliesh. I remember being unsure what my students would make of her. She looked like Agatha Christie's Miss Marple. A slightly stooping figure, she was dressed in a neat but slightly dated tweed suit, a hat and she carried a large, well-used handbag – a little lady who, one might think, would have nothing relevant to say to the youth of today. But when she stood up to speak, it was immediately evident that here was someone who had clear views and expected to be listened to. She set out how the younger generation should approach the future, what she thought they should be concerned about and what they should not, and what their underlying values should be. And she did so with a charm that was beguiling, revealing a warm and understanding nature behind a no-nonsense exterior. She was everyone's grand-mother – and she had the students eating out of the palm of her hand! I thought immediately of Frances Alguire.

I can't remember when I first met Fran. It will have been at a meeting of the World Methodist Council Executive Committee, but I can't remember which. We were certainly both at the meeting at Hotel Viktoria in Reuti-Hasliburg, Switzerland in 1989, when her husband, Don, and my wife, Sally, organized an outing for the com-mittee members' spouses. The spouses (they became known as the Spice) were to go on a trip up the Jungfrau. They had such fun on that trip, and Don and Sally got on so well that the four of us got together later for a meal. It was immediately clear to me that Fran was someone of deep faith and clear vision.

But I really got to know her when we were both began attending meetings of the Officers of the World Methodist Council, I as then Chair of the Program Committee and she as Chair of the North American Section of the World Methodist Council. Here was a lay woman who wasn't afraid to speak her mind clearly and forcefully in what was still a very male and clerical body, and it was evident that when she spoke she was listened to.

The Officers met in 1995 in Cambridge, England, and I found myself in the role of host. Towards the end of their five-day meeting, the Nominating Committee met. I remember the Rev. Dr. Donald English, then Chairperson, taking me aside and confiding to me that the Nominating Committee was going to nominate Fran Alguire as the next Chairperson of the Council, the first woman, let alone laywoman, to be nominated for the post. I recall him being at pains to explain to me what I suspect he thought might seem a surprising choice. But I wasn't surprised at all. I had already noticed Fran's leadership qualities.

Of course, Fran Alguire was not at all like her predecessors in the chair and she did not try to be. She did not try to emulate the eloquence of her immediate predecessor or the erudition of former chairpersons. She was simply herself. She would typically begin an Officers meeting with a poem or reflection in conjunction with the lighting of a candle or the passing round of smoothed pebbles collected from the sea shore and launch us into our meeting with a simple yet profound truth to hold on to.

One of the especially memorable occasions of her period in office as Chairperson was the Executive Committee Meeting in Rome in 1997. As part of it we were able to attend one of Pope John Paul II's public audiences held in St Peter's Square. The Officers were invited to special seats which would enable them to be introduced to His Holiness. I have a very vivid recollection of the warmth of his greeting of Fran and then the way in which he allowed her to lead him along the line of Officers to greet each in turn. I felt very proud of World Methodism that day for having, through her election to the

Chair of its Council, expressed so clearly Methodism's emphasis upon the importance of lay leadership.

It was while Fran was Chair that Joe Hale announced his retirement as General Secretary. She led the Council in paying tribute to Joe's remarkable service to the Council over 25 years. She also oversaw the appointment of George Freeman as his successor.

It was during the quinqennium of her chairmanship, that the Council began to review its aims and structure. I suspect she was never fully persuaded that the exercise was necessary, but it is to her credit that she not only allowed it to take place but also took an active interest in what was being discussed.

In such moments one was aware of her attention to detail. She is not one for great pomp and ceremony; she prefers things done simply but she likes things done properly and in an orderly manner. I couldn't help noticing that during committees and Council meetings, she invariably carried a handwritten list of things that needed to be done or checked that day.

But for Fran Alguire, important as are the details, much more important still is integrity. She has been brought up to recognize the value of honest endeavor, hard work and determination to see things through to a proper conclusion, and she has always looked for this in others.

She had the reputation amongst Executive and Council Members of being something of an "iron lady." Certainly she could be firm about her rulings from the chair, and maybe some thought she took this to the point of being stubborn and inflexible. But I saw a softer side. She is a very sensitive person, and her sometimes hard-seeming exterior persona conceals a vulnerability that is endearing. Privately, she was and is totally dependent on her beloved Don; he has been a rock of support on which she has depended throughout her public life.

Someone has also described Margaret Thatcher, the former British Prime Minister, as an iron lady, but "an iron lady with a firm faith and a warm heart." That phrase would make a good epitaph for Frances Alguire.

Dr. John C.A. Barrett, principal of the Anglo-Chinese School (International) in Singapore, is 2006-2011 president of the World Methodist Council.

EPILOGUE

By Dr. Frances Werner Alguire

Commit your work to the Lord, and your plans will be established.

— Proverbs 16:3 NRSV[1]

Without the support and encouragement of my dear husband, this book would not be in your library. During the five years I was elected to serve as President of the World Methodist Council many persons would ask about my travels and comment, "You should write a book." In March of 2007, Don contacted Cynthia Astle. After spending a few days with us, Cynthia agreed to do the editorial work. We are indebted to Cynthia for putting the many details in order for this volume, plus bountiful thanks to dear daughters Mary and Catherine, and to our many friends for their remembrances, which have generated fond memories of times we were serving together throughout the world.

Each of our stories and experiences are varied in the challenging, ever-changing journey called life. Now that Don and I are both octogenarians we can testify how quickly the years go by. Being actively involved in various capacities of the World Methodist Council, and with its many members, has been a life-changing experience. God has truly created an amazing multitude of males and females in the image of God. The faith, hope and love we share as followers of Jesus Christ does change lives of individuals in unbelievable ways. The work on Planet Earth is ongoing. As we continue to serve throughout this earthly garden, part of everyone's mission is to prepare others to carry on with the unfinished work. There is still much to do before peace, justice, equality and basic human needs will be available for all.

Having represented our World Methodist family on six continents and several islands, my prayers reach out to the many world residents where hunger, disease, civil strife, and warfare continue to destroy innocent lives. Life is a gift from God. The way we live each day can be a gift to others as we reach out in service.

In the words of John Wesley, an 18th century theologian who founded the Protestant Methodist movement and devoted his life to helping others:

Do all the good you can,
By all the means you can,
In all the ways you can,
In all the places you can,
At all the times you can,
To all the people you can,
As long as ever you can.

For Christians reliving God's narrative as revealed in the life of Christ, we are shown where we are to go and what we are to do as God's people. As we pray, plan, and act we are prepared to go forth as faithful servants in 'Our World Parish.' Remember God's promise:

"Fear not, for I am with you; be not dismayed;
For I am your God. I will strengthen you, yes, I will help you;
I will uphold you with my righteous right hand. "

— Isaiah 41:10 NRSV[2]

God has created each human being uniquely different. As we mature and go forth to serve, share and lead, may we not become carbon copies of others but each maintain individual authenticity.

And in the words of St. Paul, "Press On!"

Donald and Frances Alguire with their family in 2006: (front left to right) grand-daughters Erin and Anna, daughter Mary and Frances; (back left to right), daughter Catherine, grandsons Jackson and Joe and Donald.

190

References
and Chapter Notes

Frances Maxine Werner Alguire
Curriculum Vita

Professional-

Registered Nurse — served with U.S. Army Cadet Nurse Corps 1945-1948

Supervisor of General Hospital Medical/Surgical Unit 1948-50

Supervisor of General Hospital Central Supply Department 1950-1951

Public School Nurse (800 students) 1965-76.

Consultant for Leadership Development, Program Planning and Financial Development 1990-96

Co-owner, with Donald Alguire, of "Ageless Artifacts," buying and selling antiques and collectibles, 1991-96

Education

Graduate of Edward W. Sparrow Hospital School of Nursing, Lansing, MI.

Leadership Development Courses, Elgin, Illinois Community College.

Certified Lay Speaker and Mission Interpreter

Licensed Vision Screening Technician

Numerous Continuing Education Courses/Seminars in Leadership Training, Management, Theology, Speaking, Financial & Program Planning, Health Nutrition, and Disciple Bible Study.

Honorary Doctorate in Humane Letters, Adrian College, Adrian, MI.

Honorary Doctorate, Garrett-Evangelical Theological Seminary, Evanston, IL.

Church and Volunteer Service

World Methodist Council, Lake Junaluska, North Carolina

President/Chairperson 1996-2001

Honorary President/Chairperson 2001-2006

Presidium (Officers) 1991 to Present

President, North American Section, 1986-1991

Member of Executive Committee and Finance Committee 1981-1986

Delegate to Council, 1976-Present

Attended World Methodist Conferences:

Dublin 1976

Honolulu, Hawaii, 1981

Nairobi, Kenya, 1986

Singapore, 1991

Attended World Methodist Conferences (Continued):
  Rio de Janeiro, Brazil, 1996
  Brighton, England, 2001
  Seoul, South Korea, 2006
Countries and states visited during WMC service: Argentina, Australia, Belgium, Bulgaria, Brazil, China, England, Estonia, Germany, Hong Kong, India, Indonesia, Ireland, Israel, Italy, Jamaica, Kenya, New Zealand, Nigeria, Philippines, Romania, Singapore, South Africa, South Korea, Spain, Tonga, United States of America, Vatican City, West Samoa.

World Council of Churches, Geneva, Switzerland
  Adviser to Central Committee, 2001

Garrett-Evangelical Theological Seminary, Evanston, Illinois
  Board of Trustees 1973-1983
  Associate in Seminary Relations 1983-86
  Associate Director of Seminary Relations, March 1986 to July 1988

The United Methodist Church
  General Board of Global Ministries
    Director, 1976 -1984
    Ecumenical Interreligious Concerns Division 1980-84 (became the General Commission on Christian Unity and Interreligious Concerns)
    Health & Welfare Program Area 1976-80
    Africa Church Growth and Development 1976-84

  Women's Division (administrative arm of United Methodist Women)
    Director 1976-84
      Social & International Affairs Committee
      Development Education Committee
    Resource leader at 12 regional Schools of Christian Mission on College campus in five United Methodist jurisdictions 1976-84
    Financial interpreter 1985-88
    Chaired education seminar at UNESCO in Paris, France, with Follow-up fact-finding tours in Tanzania, Zambia and Kenya 1979

  General Commission on the General Conference 1980-88; Chair 1984-88
  North Central Jurisdiction Program Committee, 1976-84; Chair 1980-84
  United Methodist seminaries "Agenda 21st Century Task Force."
  General Conference delegate 1976, 1980, 1984, 1988.

North Central Jurisdiction delegate, 1976, 1980, 1984, 1988

North Central Jurisdiction Episcopal Committee 1984-88.

West Michigan Annual Conference
        Lay Member 1992-96
        Conference Personnel Committee, Secretary
        President, United Methodist Women 1992-96
        Local Church Administrative Committee
        Member, Organizational Committee, Chapel Hill UMC,
        Battle Creek, Michigan, 1957

Northern Illinois Annual Conference
        Lay Member 1964-1976
        Conference President, United Methodist Women, 1972-76
        Conference Council on Ministries
        Certified Lay Speaker
        Member, First UMC of Elgin, Illinois, 1957-1962
        Member, Hinsdale UMC, 1962-1990

North Carolina Annual Conference
        Member of Chapel Hill United Methodist Church, Chapel Hill, NC

United Nations

Delegate, 4th International Seminar, "Peaceful Uses of Atomic Energy," Geneva, Switzerland, 1971

Conference on the Decade of Women, Nairobi, Kenya, 1985
        Chaired Committee on Women & Health Strategies

European Economic Committee, Vienna, Austria, 1984, Non-Governmental Organization Observer for United Methodist Women

Appearances

Radio
World Day of Prayer Lenten series
Interviews as President of World Methodist Council, 1996-2001 in Philippines, West Samoa, Indonesia, Italy, Korea, Argentina, USA.

Television
"Women in the Church" dialogue with Bishop Paul Washburn

Presentations of World Methodist Peace Award
1996 Dr. Kofi Annan, United Nations General Secretary,
        New York, New York
1997 Prof. Andrea Riccardi, representing the Community
        of Sant'Egidio, Rome, Italy
1998 Estella Barnes de Carlotto, president, representing Grandmothers

of the Plaza de Mayo, Buenos Aires, Argentina
1999 Nelson Mandela, Capetown, South Africa
2000 Dr. Joe Hale, Brighton, England

Print

Response, the magazine of United Methodist Women
        "Local Woman — Change Agent" 1977
        "100 Years of Thank Offerings" 1981
        "Commentary on Employed Women's Consultation"
        "United Nations Prayer Card"

Personal

Married to Donald E. Alguire 1949-Present
Two daughters, Mary Frances Alguire Papish, Chicago, Illinois;
Catherine Alguire, Chapel Hill, North Carolina
Four grandchildren.

Highlights of Dr. Frances M. Alguire's 1996-2001 Term
As President of the World Methodist Council

Chaired Officers meetings:
    August 1996 — First meeting of new officers, Rio de Janeiro, Brazil
    January 1997 — Lake Junaluska, North Carolina
    September 1997 — Rome, Italy
    September 1998 — Jerusalem
    September 1999 — Hong Kong
    September 2000 — Capetown, South Africa
    July 2001   — Brighton, England

Chaired Executive Committee meetings:
    August 1996 — Organizational meeting, Rio de Janeiro
    September 1997 — Rome, Italy
    September 1999 — Hong Kong
    July 2001   — Brighton, England

Appearances:
    Community of Sant'Egidio, International Meeting of Peoples and Religions
        October 1996, Rome, Italy, "Which Humanism for 2000?"
        October 1997, Padua & Venice, Italy, "The Voice of Women
            Between Conflict & Encounter"
        September 1998, Bucharest, Romania, "The Ecumenical Movement
            in The Third Millennium."
        September, 2001, Barcelona, Spain, "A Third Millennium Without
            the Death Penalty"
    Australian Uniting Church Tricentennial Meeting, July 1997
    9th Lutheran World Assembly, Hong Kong, July 1997
    Centennial of The United Methodist Church in the Philippines, March 1998
    Dedication of Bishop William Cannon Memorial Library,
        World Methodist Council headquarters, March 1998
    International World Methodist Youth Evangelism Conference August 1998
    Adrian College "Religious Awareness Week" keynote speaker September 1998
    President Jimmy Carter's Sunday School class, Plains, Georgia, October 1998
    Meeting with Christian leaders of Jerusalem, December 1998
    Millennial Fund Dinner, General Board of Global Ministries, October 1999
    Millennium Event, North American Section, World Methodist Council
        November 1999

"Bethlehem 2000" celebration in Jerusalem, December 1999

World Circling Millennium Journey:

December 1999	Reception hosted by the queen of Tonga
	Met King of Tonga in royal dining room
Dec. 31, 1999 -	Joined 8,000 Tongas and other Pacific Islands
Jan. 1, 2000	To celebrate the turn of the millennium
	As guest of the king in the royal stands.
January 2000	Spoke at the dedication of the new Tongan
	"Free Wesleyan" headquarters building

Preached the first Sunday sermon on the
international date line in Tonga.

Presented the World Methodist Council's
Order of Jerusalem award to Dr. S. Amanaki
Havea, former Council officer, and to
The Royal Princess of Tonga for her service
with World Methodist Youth.

Honored guest at the Royal Princess and Prince
Consort's table at the 6,000-member Tonga
"Camp 2000" meeting. Greeted the group and
signed autographs.

Speaker at luncheon to honor former prime
minister of West Samoa on his 87th birthday.

Met with principal of West Samoa Pilua
Theological Seminary

Featured speaker at West Samoa Millennium
Worship service

Addressed West Samoa clergy at retreat

Gave dedication address at opening of new
building for rural West Samoa Methodist church

Escorted by West Samoa Secretary of Education
to tea with New Zealand Ambassador

January 2000	Preached at New Zealand Methodist District Evening worship on topic "Strangers No More"
	Addressed New Zealand Methodist leaders
	Addressed a Methodist group at Papanui Methodist Church in Christ Church, New Zealand
	Addressed a group of clergy at worship in Jakarta, Indonesia
	Met with then-Vice President Megawati Sukarnoputri at official residence
	Surprised by Indonesian TV for interview
	Address Indonesian Methodist Women leaders
	Met with officers of Indonesian Communion of Christian Churches
	Read Scripture at the Opening of the 4th Door of the New Millennium at St. Paul's-Outside-the-Walls to mark the start of the Week of Prayer for Christian Unity.
February 2000	Spoke at dedication of 10,000-seat Kum Nan Methodist Church in Seoul, Korea. Preached at Sunday evening service.
	Addressed Korean Methodist Church leaders.
	Interviewed by Korean Christian Broadcasting
	Addressed Korean Methodist Women
	Spoke to the National Korean Methodist Women's Choir
	Interviewed by KUK Broadcasting Radio in Seoul
July 2000	Wrote column for Methodist Recorder, newspaper of the Methodist Church of Great Britain
October 2000	Gave invocation at Garrett-Evangelical Theological Seminary Leadership Dinner
January 2001	Spoke at several Methodist churches during three-day tour of Wesley sites with Emory University theological students
	Keynote speaker for World Methodist Council Evangelism Seminar at Cliff College, UK. Led study group.

| January 2001 (Continued) | Spoke at several British Methodist Churches during weekend Evangelism event. |

| February 2001 | Served as official adviser to World Council of Churches Central Committee meeting in Potsdam, Germany |

Participated in World Council of Churches' launch of Decade to Overcome Violence
Attempted to facilitate meeting of President Bush with delegation of Christians and Muslims from Indonesia.

| March 2001 | Spoke at Hong Kong Methodist Church's 150-year celebration |

| April 2001 | Spoke at Christian Methodist Episcopal Church celebrations honoring lifetime of ministry by Bishop and Mrs. Nathaniel Linsey (on their 50th wedding anniversary). |

| June 2001 | Spoke at Virginia Annual Conference farewell to Rev. George Freeman, incoming general secretary. |

| July 2001 | Spoke at Brighton Mayor's reception for World Methodist Council Leaders |

Dedicated Christian art exhibit at Brighton University

Dedicated new building for Brighton Methodist Church

Presided at 18th World Methodist Conference, Brighton, England

Presented 2000 World Methodist Peace Award to Rev. Joe Hale, outgoing General Secretary, and Order of Jerusalem to Dr. Hale's spouse, Mary Hale, for distinguished service to the Council.

Named Honorary President upon installation of

His Eminence Sunday Mbang, prelate of the Methodist Church of Nigeria, as 2001-2006 Council President.

"A Country Girl from
a One-Room School"
Chapter Notes

1.   Alguire, Frances M., Autobiographical essay, "In the Beginning."
2.   Craig, Steve, University of North Texas, " 'The Farmer's Friend': Radio Comes to Rural America, 1920-1927" Journal of Radio Studies 2001, Vol. 8, No. 2, Pages 330-346 (doi:10.1207/s15506843jrs0802_9)
3.   Alguire, Frances M., Autobiographical essay, "In the Beginning."
4.   Astle, Cynthia B., Interview with Frances M. Alguire, March 21-23, 2007.
5.   Alguire, Frances M., Autobiographical essay, "Meet My Parents."
6.   Astle, Cynthia B., Interview with Frances M. Alguire, March 21-23, 2007.
7.   Alguire, Frances M., Autobiographical essay, "Meet My Parents."
8.   Ibid.
9.   Ibid.
10. Ibid.
11. Ganzel, Bill, Wessels Living History Farm, York, Nebraska, http://www.livinghistoryfarm.org/farminginthe30s/money_09.html
12. Alguire, Frances M. Autobiographical essay, "In the Beginning."
13. Interview notes, April 4, 2007
14. Alguire, Frances, autobiographical essay, "Post-High School."
15. Ibid.
16. The United Methodist Hymnal No. 577,"God of Grace and God of Glory," copyright 1989 by the United Methodist Publishing House, Nashville, Tennessee.
17. Fosdick, Harry Emerson, "Twelve Tests of Character," Harper & Brothers Publishers, New York and London. Copyright, 1923, by The International Committee of Young Men's Christian Associations, Chapter 10, "Magnanimity."
18. Astle, Cynthia B., Interview with Frances M. Alguire, March 21-23, 2007
19. Alguire, Frances, autobiographical essay, "On Becoming a Nurse."
20. Ibid.
21. Alguire, Frances, autobiographical essay, "March Whirl - March 5, 1948"
22. Ibid.
23. Ibid.
24. Astle, Cynthia B., Interview with Frances M. and Donald Alguire, March 21-23, 2007
25. Alguire, Donald, 50th wedding anniversary essay, "1949 to 1999."

'That Talented Lady'
Chapter Notes

1   Alguire family calendar records, compiled by Donald Alguire.
2   "1949 to 1999", 50th anniversary memoir by Donald Alguire.
3   Alguire family calendar records, compiled by Donald Alguire.
4   Astle, Cynthia B., Interview with Frances M. Alguire, March 21-23, 2007.
5   Ibid.
6   Alguire, Frances, "A Brief Summary 1958-62."
7   Ibid.
8   Ibid.
9   New Revised Version of The Holy Bible, Copyright 1989 Christian Education Committee of the National Council of Churches USA. Used by permission.
10   Alguire, Frances, "A Brief Summary 1958-62.
11   Astle, Cynthia B. Interview with Frances M. Alguire, March 21-23, 2007
12   Alguire, Frances, "Recollections of 1962-63."
13   Ibid.
14   Astle, Cynthia, Interview with Vivian Miner, May 2007
15   Alguire, Frances, "Recollections of 1962-63."
16   Ibid.
17   Astle, Cynthia B., Interview with Frances M. Alguire, March 21-23, 2007.
18   Ibid.
19   Alguire family records, compiled by Donald Alguire.
20   Astle, Cynthia B., Interview with Frances M. Alguire, March 21-23, 2007
21   "1949 to 1999", 50th anniversary memoir by Donald Alguire.
22   Personal letter of Jean Beal, May 2007
23   Alguire, Frances M., "Addendum to Celebrating the New," Northern Illinois Annual Conference Journal of United Methodist Women 1973-96.
24   Ibid.
25   Francis, Roberta W. "The History Behind the Equal Rights Amendment," ERA Task Force, National Council of Women's Organizations, http://www.equal-rightsamendment.org/era.htm
26   Ibid.
27   Ibid.
28   Astle, Cynthia B., Interview with Frances M. Alguire, March 21-23, 2007
29   Alguire, Frances, "A Continuing Journey — United Methodist Women in Northern Illinois" (1985).

"Local Woman - Change Agent"
Chapter Notes

1   Alguire, Frances M. M., "Local Woman — Change Agent," Response Magazine, June 1977.

2   "This Is Our Story," 2007 statistical report on The United Methodist Church, published by the General Council on Finance and Administration, Nashville, TN.

3   Alguire, Frances M., 1977 calendar summary.

4   Astle, Cynthia B., report on Bishop Thomas and the Central Jurisdiction, United Methodist Reporter, 1999.

5   Alguire, Frances M., 1977 calendar summary.

6   Alguire, Catherine, personal recollection, July 2007.

7   Ibid.

8   Ibid.

9   Ibid.

10   Ibid.

11.   Alguire, Frances M., 1979 calendar summary

12   Ibid.

13   Ibid.

14   Ibid.

15   Ibid.

16   Ibid.

17   Alguire, Frances M., personal reflection July 2007.

18   General Board of Global Ministries, Women's Division, World Development Program agenda, July 1979.

19   Alguire, Frances M., 1979 calendar summary

20   Ibid.

21   Ibid.

22   Western Historical Manuscript Collection, Columbia University, Papers of Rosemary Lucas Ginn, president of the United States Commission on UNESCO, http://whmc.umsystem.edu/invent/3964.html#unes1

23   Alguire, Frances M., 1979 calendar summary

24   Ibid

25   Tanzania National Website, subsection "Water," www.Tanzania.go.tz/water.html

26   Alguire, Frances M., 1979 calendar summary.

27   Ibid.

28   Wikipedia entry on Jomo Kenyatta, http://en.wikipedia.org/wiki/Jomo_Kenyatta

29   Wikipedia entry on Bronislaw Malinowski, http://en.Wikipedia.org/wiki/Bronislaw Malinowski.

30   Alguire, Frances M., 1979 calendar summary.

31   Wikipedia entry on Jomo Kenyatta,
      http://en.wikipedia.org/wiki/Jomo_Kenyatta
32   Alguire, Frances M., 1979 calendar summary.
33   Ibid.
34   Alguire, Catherine, personal recollection, July 2007.
35   Alguire, Frances M., 1979 calendar summary.
36   Alguire, Frances M., 1980 calendar summary.
37   Ibid.
38   Ibid.
39   Ibid.
40   Ibid.
41   Ibid.
42   Fulmer, Sharon, "Pioneer Marjorie Matthews "knew the call'," United
      Methodist News Service, Dec. 5, 2000, archived with Worldwide News
      Service, www.wfn.org
43   Alguire, Frances M., 1980 calendar summary.
44   Fulmer, Sharon, "Pioneer Marjorie Matthews "knew the call'," United
      Methodist News Service, Dec. 5, 2000, archived with Worldwide News
      Service, www.wfn.org
45   DeWitt, Bishop Jesse R., personal reflection, July 2007.
46   Alguire, Frances M., "Litany for Development," Aug. 8, 1980.
47   Alguire, Frances M., 1980 calendar summary.
48   Ibid.
49   Alguire, Frances M., Laity Address segment on Africa Church Growth
      and Development, Northern Illinois Conference, 1983.
50   Klemensrud, Judy, "Women's Health Discussed as a Worldwide Problem,"
      New York Times, Nov. 13, 1983
51   Ibid
52   Core Health Indicators, World Health Organization, WHOSIS database,
      http://www.who.int/whosis/database/core/core_select.cfm
53   UN Chronicle, "United Nations Decade for Women 1976-1985; 'Really only
      a beginning...' July-August, 1985, located through Look Smart,
      http://findarticles.com/p/articles/mi_m1309/is_v22/ai_3838336/pg_1
54   Salter, Andris Y., personal reflection, June, 2007.
55   Ibid.
56   Astle, Cynthia B., interview with Frances M. Alguire, March 21-23, 2007
57   United Methodist Reporter, May 1988
58   Aldersgate Celebration, North American Program
59   Ibid.
60   Astle, Cynthia B. interview with Frances and Donald Alguire,
      March 23-24, 2007
61   Ibid.

'God Trusted a Woman'
Chapter Notes

1   Alguire, Frances, "Which Humanism for 2000?" address at the International Conference on Peace and Religion sponsored by The Community of Sant'Egidio, Oct. 7-10, 1996, Rome, Italy.

2   "The Methodist Ecumenical," New York Times, September 4, 1881.

3   "The World's Methodist Council," New York Times, September 15, 1881.

4   Ibid.

5   "Methodists Are Told of Censorship Danger," New York Times, October 24, 1931.

6   "Methodists Score Rise in Racial Bias," New York Times, October 3, 1947.

7   Ibid.

8   Ibid.

9   Dugan, George, "Dedication Held for Wesley Data," New York Times, September 3, 1956.

10 Dugan, George, "Methodism Base Junaluska's Aim," New York Times, September 9, 1956.

11 Ibid.

12 Ibid.

13 Dugan, George, "President Warns of Peace Apathy," New York Times, September 1, 1956

14 "Methodist Talks Open, Conference Convenes in Oslo – Kennedy Sends Message," New York Times, August 18, 1962.

15 "Methodist Leader Hails Pope Paul on Encyclical," New York Times, August 11, 1964.

16 "Catholics to Form Unit With World Methodists," New York Times, July 19, 1966.

17 "Jersey Layman President of World Methodist Council," New York Times, August 19, 1970.

18 Astle, Cynthia, Interview with Frances M. Alguire, March 23-24, 2007.

19 Ibid.

20 "History of the World Methodist Peace Award," cached document, http://64.233.167.104/search?q=cache:xf6dRUzsmi8J:www.worldmethodist council.org/2005_peace_award_booklet.pdf+World+Methodist+ Conference+1976+Dublin,+Ireland&hl=en&ct=clnk&cd=5&gl=us

21 Ibid.

22 Kingston, Gillian, "Methodist / Roman Catholic Relations Strengthening Each Other's Hand in God," address at the Ninth Annual Conference in Honor of Father Paul Wattson and Mother Lurana White, Centro Pro Unione, Rome, Dec. 14, 2006.

23 "Methodists Elect New Top Leaders," New York Times, August 29, 1976.

24 World Methodist Evangelism Institute, "A History of the Institute," http://www.wmei.ws/history.htm
25 Evangelical Lutheran Church in America, "Ecumenical and Interfaith Relations," http://www.elca.org/ecumenical/ecumenicaldialogue/united methodist/index.html
26 Mbang, His Eminence Sunday, personal reflection July 2007
27 "1949 to 1999", 50th anniversary memoir by Donald Alguire.
28 Young, Ralph C., personal reflection, May 2007.
29 Astle, Cynthia, Interview with Frances M. Alguire, March 23-24, 2007.
30 Alguire, Frances M., Letter to Dr. Joe Hale, March 22, 1991.
31 Hale, Rev. Joe, Letter to Frances M. Alguire, March 14, 1991.
32 Wikipedia, http://en.wikipedia.org/wiki/Apartheid
33 Astle, Cynthia B., "From Hatred to Hope," United Methodist Reporter, September 2000.
34 Mogoba, Dr. M. Stanley, Letter to Frances M. Alguire, January 2002.
35 Brady, Rev. Hal, personal reflection, May 2007
36 Mbang, His Eminence Sunday, personal reflection July 2007
37 Astle, Cynthia, Interview with Frances M. and Donald Alguire, March 23-24, 2007.
38 Ibid.
39 Ibid.
40 Papish, Robert, "Ode to Women," 1996
41 Astle, Cynthia, Interview with Frances M. and Donald Alguire, March 23-24, 2007.
42 Beal, Jean, personal reflection, June 2007
43 Brady, Rev. Hal, personal reflection, May 2007
44 Young, Ralph C., personal reflection, May 2007.
45 Dutton, Rev. Denis C., personal reflection, June 2007.
46 Patterson, Ronald P., United Methodist Reporter, Aug.. 22, 1996
47 Astle, Cynthia, Interview with Donald Alguire, March 23-24, 2007.
48 Alguire, Catherine, personal reflection, July 2007
49 Astle, Cynthia, Interview with Frances M. Alguire, March 23-24, 2007.
50 Garrett-Evangelical Theological Seminary, citation conferring Doctor of Humane Letters degree upon Frances M. Alguire, June 1997.
51 Astle, Cynthia, Interview with Frances M. Alguire, March 23-24, 2007.
52 Ibid.
53 Ibid.
54 Ibid.
55 Young, Ralph C., personal reflection, May 2007
56 Greene, Linda, personal reflection, June 1, 2007.
57 Attias, Dr. Monica, personal reflection, July 2007
58 Greene, Linda, personal reflection, June 1, 2007.
59 Bullard, Mary Ellen, personal reflection, June, 2007.

60   Greene, Linda, personal reflection, June 1, 2007.
61   Ibid.
621 Mbang, His Eminence Sunday, personal reflection, July 2007
63   Greene, Linda, personal reflection, June 1, 2007.
64   Quick, Rev. William K., personal reflection, June 11. 2007
65   Nacpil, Bishop Emerito P., Letter to Frances M. Alguire, October 1997.
66   "World Parish," World Methodist Council newsletter, January-February 1998.
67   Irvins, Jim, Letter to Frances M. Alguire, January, 1998.
68   Alguire, Frances M., "An Appeal: Statement from Dr. Frances M. Alguire, Chairperson of the World Methodist Council," World Parish, January 1998.
69   Bloom, Linda, "Kofi Annan receives World Methodist Peace Award," United Methodist News Service, December, 1998.
70   Alguire, Frances M., greeting to 6th International Christian Youth Conference on Evangelism, August, 1998.
71   Jadhav, Esther, personal reflection, July 2007
72   Bloom, Linda, "World Peace Meeting Proves Timely for Religious Leaders," United Methodist News Service, September 1998.
73   Alguire, Frances M. prayer for the memorial service of Carl Baxter Collins, Bucharest, Rumania, September 1998.
74   Astle, Cynthia, Interview with Frances M. Alguire, March 23-24, 2007.
75   Alguire, Frances M., sermon for chapel service, Adrian College, Adrian, Michigan, Sept. 24, 1998.
76   Bloom, Linda, "World Methodist Officers Meet in Jerusalem," United Methodist News Service, Dec. 18, 1998.
77   World Parish, "Council Officers Meet Jerusalem Church Leaders," November-December 1998.
78   "Achieving the Vision" brochure, 1999.
79   Proceedings of the 18th World Methodist Conference, Brighton, England, 2001
80   Ibid
81   Ibid
82   Alguire, Frances M., travel itinerary, 1999.
83   World Parish, newsletter of the World Methodist Council, Spring 2000
84   Ibid.
85   Ibid.
86   Alguire, Frances M., personal remembrance, 2000
87   Ibid.
88   Ibid
89   Ibid
90   Ibid
91   World Parish, newsletter of the World Methodist Council, Spring 2000
92   Astle, Cynthia B., Interview with Frances and Donald Alguire, March 21-23, 2007.

To Brighton and Beyond
Chapter Notes

1   Proceedings of the 18th World Methodist Conference, Brighton England, 2001 "Jesus Christ, God's Way of Salvation," (pages 28-31), Lake Junaluska, NC.
2   Fox, Rev. Dr. H. Eddie, personal reflection, August, 2007.
3   Brady, Rev. Dr. Hal, personal reflection, July 2007
4   Proceedings of the 18th World Methodist Conference, Brighton England, 2001 "Jesus Christ, God's Way of Salvation," (pages 37-40), Lake Junaluska, NC.
5   Ibid.
6   Ibid, pages 73-88
7   Alvim, Dr. Gustavo Jacques Diaz, personal reflection, July 2007
8   Proceedings of the 18th World Methodist Conference, Brighton England, 2001 "Jesus Christ, God's Way of Salvation," (pages 133-269), Lake Junaluska, NC.
9   Ibid, page 148.
10 Ibid, page 104
11 Freeman, Rev. George H., personal reflection, August 2007.
12 Ibid
13 Um, Mary, personal reflection, August 2007
14 Ibid.
15 Ibid.
16 Astle, Cynthia, Interview with Frances and Donald Alguire, March 21-23, 2007.
17 Gifford, Darcy, "A World of Faith: An interview with Fran Alguire," *Contact: Adrian College Alumni Magazine*, Winter 2003.
18 Attias, Dr. Monica, personal reflection, July 2007.

Epilogue Chapter Notes

1   The Holy Bible, New Revised Standard Version, copyright 1989 by the Christian Education Committee of the National Council of Churches USA. Used by permission.
2   Ibid.

About the editor

Cynthia B. Astle has been a professional writer and editor for nearly 35 years.

 She began a journalism career in Florida, where she worked for 15 years as a reporter and editor on a series of community weeklies and mid-sized daily newspapers. In 1988, she joined the editorial staff of *The United Methodist Reporter*. In 1996, after a decade of working with the expanding Internet, she led the UMR team that developed its first online publication, *Reporter Interactive*. In 2000, she became the first woman to be named Editor of the *Reporter* in its 160-year history. She served as Editor until May 2005.

Over the past 20 years, she has reported on five General Conferences of The United Methodist Church – 1988, 1992, 1996, 2000, 2004 – and, God willing, will report on the 2008 General Conference. She attended the 1992 World Methodist Conference in Singapore and the 2001 World Methodist Conference in Brighton, England, and has covered the Council's Executive Committee and officers' meetings in Varna, Bulgaria; Rome, Italy; and Cape Town, South Africa.

Since September 2005, Cynthia has been associated with *The Progressive Christian*, a bimonthly ecumenical magazine focusing on "faith and the common good," formerly known as *Zion's Herald* magazine. In 2006 she helped launch United Methodist NeXus, www.umnexus.org, an online magazine of news, context and commentary for United Methodists. As editor, Cynthia led UM NeXus in its first year of publication to top rankings among religious "e-zines" in North America from both the United Methodist Association of Communicators and Associated Church Press. In December 2007 she was named Managing Editor of *The Progressive Christian*.

Her affiliations include the Order of St. Luke, a dispersed monastic community of women and men, lay and clergy, seeking to live a sacramental life; Phi Kappa Phi, the university academic honor society dedicated to lifelong learning; Religion Communicators' Council; and Associated Church Press, where she is 2007-2009 vice president of its international board of directors. A longtime United Methodist, she is a Certified Lay Speaker in the North Texas Annual Conference, where she is a member of St. Stephen United Methodist Church in Mesquite, Texas.

She and her husband John Astle, a computer systems administrator in the printing industry, have been married since 1976. They have an adult son, Sean Damon Astle, and reside in Dallas, Texas.

3950874